Role Play & Drama

Chris Heald

Bright Ideas
for Early Years

Published by Scholastic Publications Ltd,
Villiers House, Clarendon Avenue,
Leamington Spa, Warwickshire CV32 5PR

© 1993 Scholastic Publications Ltd

Reprinted 1993

Written by Chris Heald
Edited by Magdalena Hernas
Illustrations by Emma Brown
Photographs: John Twinning pp 5, 31, 41;
Isabelle Butchinsky p 7; Richard Butchins pp 9,
49; Bob Bray pp 21, 67; John Birdsall p 59;
Chris Kelly p 73; Stan Gamester p 87
Cover photograph by Martyn Chillmaid
Cover design by Keith Martin

Artwork by Steve Williams Design, Leicester

Printed in Great Britain
by the Alden Press Ltd, Oxford

**British Library Cataloguing in Publication
Data**
A catalogue record for this book is available from
the British Library.

ISBN 0 590 53077-1

Contents

Who shall we be today?   87

Appendix 1

Appendix 2

Introduction

What importance should we give to role-play and drama in the classroom?

There are many subjects jostling for priority in the classroom at present and the 'back-to-basics' lobby would have us believe that children are not being taught to read, write and add up any more, but are encouraged instead to play about all day by teachers who do not appreciate the importance of these basic skills.

It is my observation over many years of teaching that children learn best by modelling themselves on others who are important in their lives; thus we have children who join in with their parents' daily chores and copy the actions of making tea, washing up or hoovering; children who work in the garden with their grandparents who copy their mannerisms, for instance, straightening up with loud groans from a kneeling position.

In all societies, children copy adult role models and carry on patterns of behaviour encouraged by their society. They cannot actually *behave* like adults, since they do not have the maturity to understand adult behaviour. But they practise being adults in the sort of play which we call role-play, since it involves playing a part that is not theirs in real life.

Oral language

Where children have access to a role-play area which is slightly removed from the immediate classroom environment — in a bay or resource area rather than in the centre of the classroom — this can really help the more withdrawn children to speak to their peers with confidence. This is particularly noticeable with children whose mother tongue is other than English, who need time to experiment with language in a relaxed atmosphere.

Fostering creative writing

Thinking of a story to act out in the role-play corner is the very well-spring of creative writing. Dramatic happenings such as children being knocked down by cars and taken to hospital happen many times a day in the role-play corner. Characters are established: 'I'm the mum, you can be the baby,' and locations set: 'We're on our way to the shops.' The teacher who takes the opportunity to structure the role-play environment to link up with emergent creative writing will have a very powerful teaching tool.

Developing understanding of emotions

Role-play gives children the opportunity to experience situations and express emotions safely, without the raw immediacy of traumatic situations in real life. Empathy for others involves an understanding of how another person feels; and so in the role-play corner we may find a mother weeping bitterly for her lost child, an angry motorist whose car will not start or a happy family going to the fair.

I have often found that some children find role-play helpful in working through emotional or behavioural difficulties they may be experiencing. It was noticed after the Aberfan disaster that the young survivors enacted funerals for a considerable period following the tragedy. Such role-play may be beneficial in a therapeutic sense, allowing the stylised and harmless expression of such emotions as anger, sorrow, jealousy and hatred which society tends to look upon with disfavour.

Confidence

When the concept of role-play is extended to include a performance for an audience, there is no doubt that the ability to perform in public boosts a child's self-confidence. Extroverts will, of course, find little difficulty speaking or singing in front of others, but they must not be the only children who ever perform! For the shy, quiet child the enabling teacher will provide occasions for performance which are out of the limelight, such as manipulating a puppet while another child speaks, miming some simple actions to a song or dancing with several other children. Not everyone wants to be a soloist and a large part of ensuring a successful dramatic performance is to build it around individual children's capabilities.

Role-play and drama are important for the development of the whole child, but as with any creative activity, the skilled teacher will also provide opportunities for talent and aptitude to develop and make themselves known.

Fairy tales

Chapter one

These well-loved tales form part of our earliest memories. Their familiarity to adult and child alike gives a sense of security and continuity which helps a young child feel confident enough to join in with whoever is telling the story. They are also high-interest stories, appealing to more or less everyone, but especially to young children. In a word, they are fun!

I make no apologies for starting each activity in this chapter with a reference to a book to read to the children. After all, telling a good story is the very root of drama.

The Gingerbread Man/The Chapatti Man

Topics
Food; The family of man.

Starting point
This story can be told in its traditional British form of the Gingerbread Man or adapted as a story about the Chapatti Man in schools with a high proportion of Asian pupils. It works well with any kind of bread, cake or pancakes, to suit whatever your pupils would most identify with (e.g., pitta or bagel).

What you need
A written form of your story — several published versions are available, for example, *The Gingerbread Man* edited by Vera Southgate (Ladybird Books) or *The Gingerbread Man* by David Wood (Young Puffin Books). To turn the story into that of the Chapatti Man, change the animals to an elephant, a cow, a horse, a tiger and a clever monkey who eventually eats the Chapatti Man. (For a simple version of the story see Appendix 1, page 93.)

Costumes for the animal characters are easiest made as hats (see The Three Little Pigs, page 15). The Chapatti Man can wear a large, round sandwich board made of card. The Gingerbread Man could wear a brown leotard or tights and a polo-necked jumper, decorated with cardboard 'currants'.

What to do
It is often best to start work on a dramatic production during storytime in the classroom. It allows you to try out different stories to see which one really brings out the best in the children,

everyone can 'have a go' and the most appropriate performers can be selected for the main parts. Many children feel much more secure as part of a group, so remember to stress the vital role of the performers who chant 'Run, run, as fast as you can . . .' as children need to feel that their contribution is just as important as the speaking solos.

For a class assembly or other performance, try to ensure that there is enough room for the Chapatti Man/ Gingerbread Man to run around the hall while the children chant 'Run, run . . .'. All the meetings can take place on the stage area. If there are movable stage blocks, consider placing them in the middle of the audience. If you do this, do not forget to change any established seating patterns so that the smallest children are in the middle of the audience, nearest the stage.

It is very interesting and enlightening for children to hear the two stories told at the same time, with one group enacting the Chapatti Man and the other telling the same part of the story of the Gingerbread Man. Each group should take turns to move the story on, emphasising the similarities and differences between the two versions.

Jack and the Beanstalk

Topics
Growing things; Big and little.

Starting point
Read the story of Jack and the Beanstalk, There are several versions published by Ladybird Books of which the large book is clear and concise, while the read-it-yourself one is ideal for children.

Encourage the children to talk about the story – what do they know about giants? Do they know if beans can really grow into the sky? Are giants real? Are they good or bad? What would the children do if they met a giant? What would the giant do?

What you need

A role-play area which can be made into a giant's castle in the following way: measure a large piece of card to fit right across the entrance (the corrugated kind used for wrapping furniture is excellent as it requires minimum support). Cut crenellations and a large archway to make it look like a castle. The children will enjoy painting the castle dark grey in relays and, once a sign saying 'Giant's castle' is attached, the illusion is established. An effective beanstalk can be made from old tights knotted together, decorated with either green felt or green tissue-paper leaves, depending on how much it is going to be used. Try to

provide something by way of costumes for getting into character. Tabards are easily made and reusable. We made green for Jack and his friends, and brown for the giant. Jack's mother's costume can be simply a skirt, while the seller of beans needs a cloak of some sort. You will also need some gold coins made from gold foil and cardboard. And some beans, of course.

What to do

Encourage the children to take the parts of the characters in the story and even to invent their own characters. The role-play corner should then be left for the children to play at being Jack climbing up the beanstalk to the world of the giants.

As follow-up activity, you could plant beans in jars lined with moist blotting paper to see how high they will grow. If you have a garden, plant them out for the summer, so that the children can see how a real beanstalk grows. Use runner beans for the best effect.

The Three Bears

Topics
Tell me a story; Sizes.

Starting point
If children in your class are old enough to know the story of The Three Bears well, ask them to tell it to you in their own words with the help of questions such as the following: who went to the three bears' cottage? Why was she called Goldilocks? What did she do when she saw the door was open? What was on the table?, etc. If your children are too young or too inexperienced to answer these questions, there are lots of versions of the story to choose one suitable for your class.

What you need
Three teddy bears (small, medium and large) and a doll with long blond hair.

What to do
In a relaxed way, at storytime, ask for volunteers to be the bears and Goldilocks. Demonstrate what you want the children to do by holding each toy on your knee and speaking in an appropriate voice — deep for Daddy Bear, squeaky for Baby Bear. Children find it reassuring if the performers sit on chairs while the audience sits on the floor.

If you have a confident reader who can read the story while others hold the toys in their laps, so much the better; otherwise read out the story and encourage the different characters to join in at the appropriate times. As the children become more confident,

encourage them to lift up their teddy or doll when it is their turn to speak, so that the voice really appears to be coming from the toy.

If you wish to use this approach for a class assembly or some other form of performance, consider providing more walk-on parts by allocating the porridge bowls, chairs and beds to be brought on- and off-stage.

For a full-blown performance, it is very easy to transform the play house into the cottage of the Three Bears. All you need are bowls, chairs and beds of three different sizes, a long blond wig and headbands with ears for the bears. This may well be the most appropriate, unpressured way for young children to explore the dramatic potential of a story or a situation.

The Three Little Pigs

Topics
Materials; Homes.

Starting point
Find a suitable version of the story to read to your class. Talk about the story and the reasons why the first two building materials were unsatisfactory. If you could provide samples of straw, twigs and bricks for the children to handle during the discussion, so much the better. Ask them why they think the straw and twigs were not successful, and why the bricks were the best.

NB This story as it stands should not be used with Muslim or Jewish pupils as it will give great offence to them and to their families because of religious attitudes towards pigs. In this case, the story can easily be changed to the three little lambs, goats or ducks.

What you need
Provide three pink pig head-dresses for the three pigs, and a head-dress with long black ears for the wolf. Make these

from coloured activity paper – black and grey for the wolf, pink and grey for the three pigs. First cut a strip of paper to fit around your characters' heads and staple the ends together to form a circlet. Then cut the shape of ears with linings (see illustration).

Finally, staple the ears to the headband. You could also make piggy noses from sections of an egg-box painted pink, with two large dots for nostrils. Attach elastic and you have one recognisable pig!

What to do

The children will want to join in as you read the story, especially in the repetitive dialogue between the wolf and the pigs.

If you leave the head-dresses in the role-play corner, the children will play at 'Three Little Pigs' very happily.

This story can be very successful when some of the children speak in chorus, the non-speaking actors mime actions, while the class as a whole recites the rhyming parts (for example, 'Not by the hair on my chinny-chin-chin, I will not let you in!'). A narrator or a group of narrators can tell the story outline.

The difficulty of having only a small number of parts can be got around by allocating children for the houses of straw, twigs and bricks. Three children in cardboard sandwich-boards, holding the roof, make very effective houses which blow down on cue.

pink paper ear

grey lining

black paper ear (staple onto headband)

staples

pink paper circlet

black paper circlet (measure on child's head before stapling)

egg-box section piggy nose

The Little Red Hen

Topics
Harvest; Food.

Starting point
The story of the Little Red Hen is available in many versions. Most school libraries will have the Margot Zemach edition (Hutchinson) which is on the National Curriculum reading list and is another simple-but-good rendition of an old tale. Read the story to the children, encouraging them to join in whenever possible. While some children are full of confidence and have few difficulties speaking to an audience, a great many are very shy at first and need to watch other children perform before they can try to do it themselves. I strongly believe that a tradition needs to be established within a school, so that the younger children realise that next year or the year after that, their class will be expected to provide the majority of the solo performers, and they will then be keen to participate.

What you need
Headbands with ears for the Rat, the Cat and the Dog (see The Three Little Pigs, page 15), while the same sort of headband but with a beak will work for the Little Red Hen (see illustration).

The Little Red Hen needs to have props to match the progress of the story, e.g., a trowel for planting the wheat; a watering can for watering it; shears or long scissors for harvesting; a trug full of wheat for grinding; a large bag with 'FLOUR' on it for baking. The cake can be made by covering a large circular tin with brown or yellow paper and decorating it to look like a cake. You may also need large ears of corn painted or drawn on card.

What to do

You will need to decide whether you will read out the story yourself, or get several children to read parts of the story aloud and whether to have the main parts spoken or mimed. (Miming is easier for very young children.) Once you have decided on your method of narration, you can allocate the parts from the list of characters.

List of characters
The Little Red Hen
The Rat
The Cat
The Dog
The Miller
The Baker

If extra walk-on parts are required, the Grains of Wheat can be children who gradually lift up ears of corn painted on card, as if growing.

The Enormous Turnip

Topics

Growing things; Large and small.

Starting point

Having checked first that you remember it correctly, tell the story to the children in your own words, using plenty of gestures and facial expressions. I have found this method to be most successful with younger children and it makes a pleasant change from reading from a book, being more immediate and direct communication. To emphasise the links between reading, listening and writing, you could record yourself telling the story and write it down in a 'book' for the children to read along. They can then listen to the teacher's familiar voice and see the spoken words transformed into print.

What you need

Confidence in your own abilities and those of your class! Costumes for the human characters are straightforward; for the animals you can make headbands (see Three Little Pigs, page 14). For the turnip itself, you can use a sit-on bouncing toy such as a Space Hopper (often bright orange with a face on). Attach green paper leaves to the top, turn the 'face' away and there you have an acceptable enormous turnip! We hid ours in a gap at the back of the staging-blocks, so that it looked as if it were buried in the ground.

What to do

Take the children through the story, encouraging them to use their own words to describe what happened. Ask questions like: 'What did the old man do then?' and 'Who took hold of the cat's tail?'

I prefer to leave the dialogue of this story in its oral form, calling on the children's oral memory to replay it (perhaps with slight variations each time). If you feel this would not work for your class, you could jot down what they say on a blackboard or flip-chart and create your own script.

You need to establish a pattern of actions and gestures which each character in turn uses. When one character addresses another, he or she needs to make a beckoning movement, as well as speak. The best bit, of course, is when they all fall over and the turnip comes up! Please make sure that the children realise that the audience will laugh as I have known children to dissolve into tears because they thought they were being laughed at! Once they know that it is clever to make people laugh, they are perfectly happy for it to happen.

The Golden Goose (The Princess Who Could Not Smile)

Topics
People; Happy and sad.

Starting point
This story is ideal for extempore drama. It is useful both for an assembly and for a class story/drama session. It can also be used as part of a performance for parents. Read or tell the story to the class, asking the children to think about what they would do to make the story come to life. Published versions of the story include *The Golden Goose* by Betty Evans (Ladybird Books) and *The Golden Goose* by the Grimm Brothers (Award Publications).

What you need
A copy of the story (see Appendix, page 95, for a simple version). You will also need crowns for the king, the princess and Jack, and a headband with a beak for the goose (see illustration on page 16).

What to do
Tell the children that you are looking for volunteers to act out the story. Then either tell/read the story to the children or give them a brief synopsis and then encourage participation as you read/tell the full story for the first time. I prefer the second approach as it has more immediacy, and children, swept up in the action, lose their self-consciousness.

Synopsis
There was once a princess who was always sad, so her father offered her hand in marriage to the man who could make her laugh. A boy called Jack found a golden goose which made everyone who touched it stick together in a long line. When the princess saw this, she laughed for the first time, and Jack married her and became a prince.

Give the hats to the volunteers, letting them know which character they are to play, then tell/read the story and let them join in turn. If there is time, this can be done two or three times with different sets of children, without boredom setting in.

It is obviously better for a performance if the children themselves can be responsible for the narrative links. With really young children this is not usually feasible, so perhaps in these cases you could 'borrow' some older children, thus giving the younger ones some role models of successful speakers/readers whose efforts can be emulated in a year or so.

To give your performance a twist, you could introduce staff members as the followers of the golden goose. This obviously needs to be done with tact and diplomacy but it will allow the children's skill at mimicry to display itself.

The Old Woman and Her Pig

Topics
Animals; The countryside.

Starting point
Read the story to the children. The Ladybird version by Vera Southgate is a classic, although its small size is not ideal for working with a whole class. Kookaburra Books do a larger version written by Mary O'Toole which is easier for a child to read.

NB For schools with a large Muslim or Jewish population, for whom stories about pigs are unacceptable, change the stubborn animal into a donkey and it will read just as well.

What you need
Costumes for this story would be rather difficult, not to say impossible, but you can get around this by having each child who takes part hold a placard depicting the character he or she is playing (see illustration).

What to do
The largest speaking part is the Old Woman — a group of children could take it in turns to play her. Depending on the age of the children, a lot of fun can be had lifting the placards up and down in the correct parts of the story. Mistakes merely add to the hilarity for the audience. The children who hold the placards can also tell the story, but if you want to extend the numbers of children involved, each character can have its own separate 'voice' standing alongside. This caters for differing levels of confidence in performing in public. All the 'voices' need to do is to first say 'No!' and shake their heads when the old woman asks for their help, and then shout 'Ouch! Ouch!' when their turn comes to be quenched, burned or beaten.

Work experience

Chapter two

We are all very conscious of demands on education from employers who want well-motivated and economically-aware youngsters in the workplace. One way in which a sense of the realities of the world of work can be fostered in young children, without compromising early years principles, is to set up role-play areas structured around particular types of workplace. The National Curriculum in Speaking and Listening, AT1 Level 1, expects children to:

'. . . participate as speakers and listeners in group activities including imaginative play.'

To make the point even stronger, the *Non-statutory Guidance for Speaking and Listening in the Classroom*, 3.3 states:

'In the classroom, the home corner can be a most valuable context for talk, particularly if developed through role-play, for example, as "hospital", "library", "ticket office", "spaceship" or "café".'

It must be stressed, however, that it takes time and opportunity to build up the sort of resources needed to provide convincing workplace play areas, which then have to be stored while they are not in use.

The hair salon

Topics

Wet and dry; Ourselves.

Starting point

Ask the children to draw a picture of the child who is sitting next to them. With very young children, this activity can concentrate on hair colour, nose, mouth and correct numbers of eyes, rather than any detail. There will still be those who choose to colour their friend's hair purple or green for reasons best known to themselves. If this happens, just point out that their friend's hair is actually brown or blond and encourage the child to discuss the difference between the picture and the real person.

What you need

Empty, clean plastic containers of perming solution, shampoo, conditioners, etc.; large plastic unbreakable mirrors (in our case borrowed from the science resources); brushes and rollers; plastic bowls for 'washing' hair; cardboard

scissors; overalls for the 'hairdressers' and gowns for the 'clients'; wigs; paper, pens and pencils.

What to do

A visit to your local hairdressing salon would make an ideal start to this activity. If this is not possible, investigate contacts among parents to see if there is a hairdresser among them who would be willing to come into school and do a demonstration. This is particularly successful if one of the staff and two of the children can have their hair done in some way, even if it is only to have a fringe trimmed.

Allow the children to decide who will be staff and who will be customers. Every opportunity should be taken to encourage emergent literacy skills by providing pens, pencils and pads for the children to make appointments.

The customers will be wearing wigs, so allow the hairdressers to brush and comb as much as they like, without causing any pain or horribly tangled hair. We only have cardboard scissors in our hairdresser's, since we have found that despite careful explanations and dire warnings, a young child's first thought is to cut large lumps out of each other's hair, given half a chance.

The travel agent

Topics

Other lands; Holidays.

Starting point

When you have made the decision to turn your role-play area into a travel agent's, discuss with the children what a travel agent does. You can ask them what resources you will need and where to get them. Parents who work in a travel agency are an excellent source of the things you will need and most families will have one or two brochures lying around the house. A visit would be a really good stimulus but this is not always possible, so consider inviting someone from your local travel agency into school to talk to the children about their job.

What you need

Several copies of a few brochures, as well as lots of single ones; posters to put on the walls (these can be designed and produced by the children themselves); telephones; a computer terminal; booking forms (these could be designed by the children themselves as a technology activity); staff uniforms. We

were very lucky in having several matching sets of scarves and hats from an ex-stewardess, which our 'agents' wear when they take their turn behind the counter.

What to do

Ask the children to establish a system for booking a holiday, collecting the booking forms into a file and making out tickets for the customers. They might like to make 'Special Offer' notices for places they have seen in the brochures or visited themselves. Do encourage the use of realistic prices. No one goes to Disneyland for £5!

Carpentry corner

Topics

Natural materials; Homes.

Starting point

Discuss the properties of wood with your children. Ask them if they know where it comes from, how it is used and what sorts of things are made from it. Talk about the different ways in which pieces of wood can be held together (glue, joints, nails, screws).

What you need

A toolbench or some other surface that can be marked with nail-holes; hammers — small pinhammers are best; a large supply of variously shaped pieces of wood (contact your local DIY shop for offcuts); pounds of 2-inch nails with heads and various screws; small screwdrivers; a drill to drill holes in some bits of wood (this has to be supervised or done by an adult).

What to do

For safety reasons, you will need to supervise this activity throughout.

Invite the children (in pairs) to join two pieces of wood. Inevitably, the pieces that have been painstakingly drilled with holes for the screws will end up being used for the nails, but this could become a source of discussion about why screws need holes drilled for them while nails do not.

Suggest that the children make either an aeroplane or a boat (see illustration), after they have been allowed to

experiment freely without a particular end in view.

THIS IS A VERY NOISY ACTIVITY! I have always found it best done out of doors in the summer.

Be prepared for the occasional banged thumb, but once they get the knack, children love this activity and will happily hammer away, filling their piece of wood with nails. This is a particularly soothing activity for aggressive children, who are able to vent their aggression on the nails and wood in a harmless fashion.

The office

Topics
Getting the message; People at work.

Starting point
It would be relatively easy to arrange a visit to your school office to look at all the things that office workers need. Talk to the children about what goes on in an office. Ask them if they know anyone who works in one.

What you need
A desk, preferably with drawers; a typewriter, a telephone, a filing cabinet and alphabetical-order files (if possible); several pairs of spectacle frames without lenses to help children 'get into character'; a large supply of paper, envelopes, various types of forms, paper-clips, pens, pencils, elastic bands, erasers, sponge pads, office stamps, rubber thimbles, telephone message pads.

What to do
Encourage the children to use the equipment appropriately. Leave a pad and pencil next to the telephone for messages. A notice-board where typing can be displayed is always popular. Nursery children can be encouraged to use their emergent writing skills in the office, but older children could use the 'office' as a study area to support their more advanced reading and writing skills. Provide a word bank and computer back-up for story-writing and you will tap into a strong vein of productive, self-motivated play.

The post office is an alternative office environment.

The garage

Topics

Transport; Machines.

Starting point

A visit to your local garage is usually fairly easy to arrange and can be full of interest for the children. Most children have called at a garage for petrol when out in their parents' car, but few will have had the chance to see the cars being repaired.

What you need

The most difficult thing to obtain is a car. If you cannot beg or borrow a pedal-car of some sort, you could consider a soap-box cart or a car made from one of the large construction sets such as Quadro or Gymbo.

You will need all the tools (real or pretend) that a mechanic uses. We have a set of real tools which have been rendered safe by removing all the pointed and dangerous parts, but this would be an expensive purchase. Plastic tools are quite acceptable and come as part of construction sets such as Brio-Mec and Bau-play.

Overalls should be provided, and the scene should be set with empty boxes of spare parts and a couple of bicycle wheels on an up-ended frame, which the children can take to pieces and put together again as they wish.

Petrol pumps can be made from cardboard boxes to which tubing is attached. A telephone, a notepad and a pen should be available for booking customers' cars in and out. Sets of old keys are also useful, especially if they are accompanied by tie-on name-tags.

What to do

Let the children look at a real car – this will usually be yours! Open the bonnet and show them the engine, pointing out all the different parts which all have to work together for the car to run properly. Encourage the children to set up a system for servicing a car, making sure that all the jobs that need doing are done by someone. It might help to design a checklist for each car. The children could then decide what needs to be done and at what price.

As always, a little adult participation is a great motivator for young children, but allow them to organise the role-play area in their way, and encourage independence and spontaneity.

The health club

Topics

My body; Leisure.

Starting point

Encourage the children to talk about the exercise they take. Many young children nowadays do not get enough exercise and are unable to run or jump for any great length of time. School trips show that walking is also something unfamiliar in their world, with requests to be carried often starting within 100 yards of the start of the walk. It is therefore important to encourage fitness, so a gymnasium or a health club should make an appearance for half a term in each role-play area in turn.

What you need

A health club needs certain types of equipment which can be rather expensive to buy. We were fortunate to be given a rowing machine, an exercise bike and a punchball by the friends of the school. We then purchased a small second-hand trampoline and light plastic dumbells. Skipping ropes from the PE stock were also used. We obtained exercise posters from our local Health Education Council, and begged and borrowed leotards, sweatbands, shorts, etc., from staff and parents. You will also need a telephone, paper and pencils to receiving 'bookings', and a cassette recorder with tapes suitable for aerobic dancing.

What to do

Lay down strict rules about using the gym apparatus, so that the children realise they could harm themselves if they do not follow them. Proper supervision is absolutely essential if this activity is to be performed safely.

Limit the numbers to a maximum of four children at a time and encourage them to book their visits in advance. One child could be the receptionist who takes telephone bookings and writes them down on the list. If possible, provide a cassette recorder with suitable tapes and encourage the children to work out dance routines for themselves.

The police station

Topics

Our town; People who help us.

Starting point

Local police stations are usually only too pleased to let young people visit their premises. Sometimes they even allow the children to go into the cells to see what it is like to be arrested. If there are organisational difficulties, you could use *Cops and Robbers* by Allan and Janet Ahlberg (Little Mammoth), as a starting point. Some very interesting impressions of what the police are for can come from class discussions.

What you need

Toy helmets, handcuffs and truncheons are widely available from toy shops. If you can get hold of some fluorescent material, you could make tabards which look a bit like the ones the police wear when dealing with traffic on the motorway. You will also need the usual office equipment such as telephone, notepads, pen, etc., and a set of large keys on a key ring for locking and unlocking the jail and the handcuffs. A large cardboard box decorated to look like a police van is a good source of dramatic play.

What to do

Talk to the children about why people can be arrested. Encourage them to designate an area of the police station as a cell and equip it accordingly. Older children should be encouraged to write a story to be acted out in the role-play area.

The café

Topics

Healthy eating; Food.

Starting point

The best way to start this role-play activity is to take the children to your local café for a visit. If this is not possible, ask your children to bring into school any badges, hats or other mementoes of their last visit to a café or a restaurant with their parents. Alternatively, read *Mrs Wobble the Waitress* by Allan Ahlberg (Young Puffin Books) and ask the children to tell you what they know about cafés.

What you need

A table (or tables, if possible), plastic or paper cutlery and crockery, white aprons, white frilly hats, bow ties, a cash register and some money, pads and pencils for the orders to be written down, stiff card for the menus; materials to make the 'food' such as cut-out pictures of food items, yellow and white foam, gummed paper, coloured acetate, tissue paper, cake tins or mousse cartons, felt-tipped pens, glue, scissors.

What to do

Ask the children to discuss what they will serve in their café. They should then prepare a few copies of the menu. They will need to decide on realistic prices for their menu.

They will have great fun making all the food for their café. Nursery children will enjoy sticking pictures of their favourite foods on to paper plates to make menu 'dishes'. Older children can make sandwiches out of triangles of thin white foam with a line drawn along the side in an appropriate colour for the filling (see illustration). Attractive cakes and tarts can be made by wrapping acetate or gummed paper around cake tins or mousse cartons, or decorating circles of yellow sponge with crumpled tissue paper or coloured acetate.

The children will need to decide who will be customers and who will wait on them. The waiters and waitresses should ensure that their customers are served promptly and politely.

Songs as a medium of drama

Chapter three

Young children love to sing and, especially if the song is accompanied by actions, seem reassured by the framework of the song and have few reservations about joining in. I have always found songs to be a suitable basis for an infant performance, especially as a way of including every child, either as a soloist or as a member of the choir.

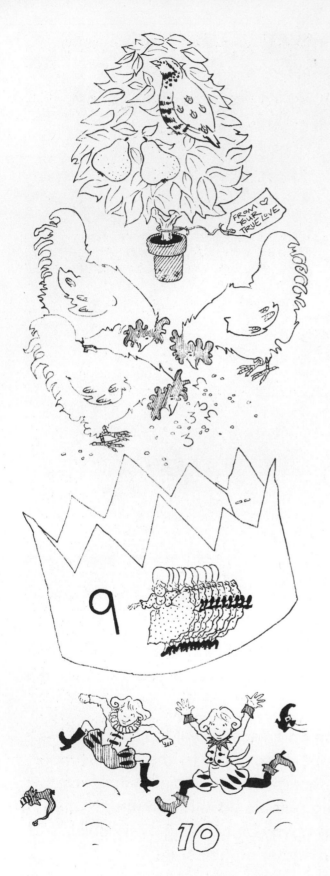

The twelve days of Christmas

Topics
Festivals; Sounds.

Starting point
Discuss the words of the song with the children, making sure that they understand the old-fashioned language used in the song. Learn the song together, one verse at a time.

What you need
A medley of musical instruments matched up to the verses as in the following example.

A partridge in a pear tree	a quack
Two turtle-doves	bird warbler
Three French hens	maraccas
Four colly birds	Guiro
Five gold rings	triangle struck five times
Six geese a-laying	squeeze-bulb horn
Seven swans a-swimming	afuche/cabasa
Eight maids a-milking	xylophone trill
Nine ladies dancing	tambourine
Ten lords a-leaping	Swannee whistle
Eleven pipers piping	kazoo
Twelve drummers drumming	snare-drum

You will also need hats for each of the twelve days. These are easily made from a band of thin card decorated with an appropriate picture on the front, with the appropriate number of overlapping outlines of turtle-doves, French hens, etc.

(see illustration). If the headbands can be cut into the shape of crowns, this looks better than plain strips.

What to do

Ask for six girls and six boys to act as volunteers to wear the crowns. You will need volunteers to play the instruments, too.

As the song is sung, the children should play the chosen instruments in a short space after each character is named; for example, 'Five gold rings' – pause while triangle is struck five times.

As their verse is sung, the person wearing the appropriate crown steps forward and either curtseys or bows (nursery children could stand up when it is their turn but would probably need help with the instruments).

This song and its actions are very effective as part of a Christmas production.

Polly put the kettle on

Topics

Hot and cold; How we used to live.

Starting point

This song has always proved a favourite with nursery and reception classes, particularly when there were large numbers of young children whose mother tongue was not English. Talk about how tea is made in their house and discuss the safety aspects of contact with boiling water.

What you need

A toy kettle (or a real one, empty), a toy hob of some kind, possibly borrowed from the play house, role-play furniture.

What to do

Ask the children if they know what 'putting the kettle on' means (the water will get hot because of the heat from the hob). Then ask what they think 'taking the kettle off' means.

Sing the rhyme with the children, picking out a child to be Polly and another one to be Sukey.

Polly put the kettle on,
Polly put the kettle on,
Polly put the kettle on,
   We'll all have tea.

Sukey take it off again,
Sukey take it off again,
Sukey take it off again,
   They've all gone away.

Repeat until everyone has had a turn.
This is a very simple performance, which should help the children to feel confident in their own abilities.

To develop this activity, ask the children to tell you how to make a cup of tea. Make it clear that you are asking them for detailed instructions which you are going to follow to the letter. If you then follow their instructions (using cool water for safety reasons) it can cause much hilarity when a vital stage (e.g., 'Put the tea in the teapot') is left out.

Older infants could draw a sequence of pictures directing a friend to make a pot of tea.

Three currant buns

Topics
Harvest; Money.

Starting point
This is a well-known song which is very suitable for use at storytime in a relaxed setting. All the children will want to take part in turn.

It is possible to use this song as part of a performance for parents based on the theme of 'Number three'. The complete

performance could include 'Three Little Speckled Frogs', 'Three Little Ducks (went swimming one day)', 'Three Green Bottles', 'Three Elephants', etc.

Any counting song can be adapted to fit your theme.

What you need
Three large cardboard pictures of currant buns, covered in sticky-backed plastic and used regularly whenever you sing this song. This gives the children something to hold, which makes them more confident performers. After all, there are professional actors who might find it difficult to 'be' a currant bun, and this activity is intended for three- to six-year olds! A baker's hat is useful for the baker. You will also need plastic pennies for the bun-buyers.

What to do

Choose the currant buns, the buyers and the baker. Give out plastic pennies to the buyers, so that they can explore the concept of exchange. Sing the song and encourage the children to perform appropriate actions.

Three currant buns in the baker's shop
  [the 'buns' step forward]
Big and round with sugar on the top.
  [all three describe a big circle with their
  hands and tap the 'icing']
[Jamie] came with his penny one day
  (a chosen child goes up to the baker]
He bought a currant bun
  [pays the baker]
And he took it right away.
  [leads a 'currant bun' away]

There are seven parts in this version, so you will need to sing it several times if everyone is to have a turn. You can, of course, use five currant buns, which raises the number of participants to eleven.

I know an old lady who swallowed a fly

Topics

Farm animals; Minibeasts.

Starting point

Sing the traditional song until it is familiar to the children. The book of the same name, published by Child's Play and illustrated by Pam Adams is a useful visual aid while you sing. Practise making the sounds of the insects and animals mentioned in the song.

What you need

A Guiro, a bird-warbler or some pan pipes, children who are good at making animal noises, a place where a lot of noise will not disturb others.

This approach has the great advantage of not needing costumes, although they would add to the visual effect of the song.

What to do

Stand your volunteers in a line, starting with the child who can buzz loudly like a fly. The song then proceeds as follows:

I know an old lady who swallowed a
    fly
    [pause for fly to buzz]
I don't know why she swallowed a fly.
    [pause for buzz]
Perhaps she'll die.

I know an old lady who swallowed a
    spider,
    [pause for Guiro]
That wriggled, and jiggled and tickled
    inside her.
    [pause for Guiro]
She swallowed the spider
    [Guiro till end of verse]
To catch the fly.
    [fly buzzing till end of verse]
I don't know why she swallowed a fly.
Perhaps she'll die.

I know an old lady who swallowed a
    bird.
    [pause for warbler]
How absurd, to swallow a bird!
    [pause for warbler]
She swallowed the bird
    [warbler till end of verse]
To catch the spider,
    [Guiro joins warbler]
That wriggled, and jiggled and tickled
    inside her.
She swallowed the spider to catch the
    fly.
    [fly joins warbler and Guiro]
I don't know why she swallowed the
    fly.
Perhaps she'll die.

The song goes on accumulating a cacophony of moos, bleats, barks, miaows, etc. The children find this highly amusing and so will any audience you may attract. 'Old MacDonald had a farm', can be performed in a very similar way.

One, two, three, four, five/Once I caught a fish alive

Topics
Leisure; Seas and Rivers.

Starting point
It is a sad fact that many children enter nursery and school not knowing many of the old nursery rhymes. Sing this song with your class over and over for a half-term or so during storytime, to make sure that they know it well. The song works perfectly well with a group of children sitting on a carpet and counting on their fingers, but it can be 'dressed up' to form part of a performance.

What you need
Sticks and string to act as fishing rods for eleven fishermen, numbers 1–10 on cardboard, ten fish shapes, one larger fish with no number on it, costumes for fishermen — we found felt hats, body warmers and large wellies worked very well.

What to do
Ask the children to make eleven fishing rods and to attach all the fish, including the blank one, to the lines. Stand the fishermen in a line with the blank-fish holder in the middle. Start with all the fish on the floor. Practise singing the song fairly slowly so that each of the fishermen can raise his or her line when the right number is called.

> One, two, three, four, five,
> Once I caught a fish alive,
> Six, seven, eight, nine, ten,
> Then I let it go again.
> Why did you let it go?
> Because it bit my finger so.
> Which finger did it bite?
> This little finger on the right.

The teacher should help by standing at the front and pointing to each child when it is their turn. The person in the middle has to demonstrate that their fish is alive by wiggling it at the end of the line. To 'let it go', the child should grab the fish and put it on the floor, then hop about waggling his or her (hopefully) right little finger.

You can sing the song at least twice, but even so this is a short performance and should be combined with other acts if greater length is required. It would be excellent as the reception class contribution to a whole-school production.

Lazy Mary

Topics
Food; Time.

Starting point
Teach your children the traditional song to the tune of 'Here we go round the mulberry bush'. Please do not wait until you are rehearsing a public performance to teach the children the songs they need to know. I have always made a point of building the performance around songs which the children already know well and love to sing.

What you need
The words to the song.

CHORUS

Mum	Lazy Mary, will you get up, will you get up, will you get up? Lazy Mary, will you get up, will you get up today?
Lazy Mary	What'll you give me if I get up, if I get up, if I get up? What'll you give me if I get up, if I get up today?

Mum [spoken]	A nice egg for your breakfast.
Lazy Mary [thinks]	Mmmmmm. No, Mother, I won't get up, I won't get up, I won't get up. No, Mother I won't get up, I won't get up today.

Mother goes away and returns later.
Repeat Chorus

Mum [spoken]	A nice pie for your dinner.
Lazy Mary [thinks]	Mmmmmm. No, Mother, I won't get up, etc.

Repeat Chorus

Mum [spoken]	A nice salad for your tea.
Lazy Mary [Repeat]	No, Mother, etc.

Repeat Chorus, this time sounding angry.

Mum	A glass of cold water all over you, if you don't get up!
Lazy Mary [thinks]	I will get up. Yes, Mother, I will get up, I will get up today!

38

You will also need a pretend bed and a nightdress for Mary and an apron for Mum.

What to do

Sing the song, encouraging one child to be Lazy Mary and another to be Mum. If either character feels confident enough, ask them to sing their part solo. Children love singing this song and it is quite acceptable to change Mum to Dad and Mary to Harry if equal opportunities issues arise.

Five elephants went out one day

Topics

The Zoo; Heavy and light.

Starting point

Make sure that your children know the words of the song. This is a popular storytime song and most enjoyable as such. It can be used very successfully as part of a performance.

What you need

The words of the song:

One elephant went out one day
On a piece of string to play.
He had such enormous fun,
He asked another elephant to come.

Two elephants . . . etc.

Either help the children to make elephant masks (see illustration) or provide large cut-out pictures of elephants for them to hold. The cut-out elephants have the advantage of being reusable if covered with sticky-backed plastic. They can then be used during storytime too. You will also need a long piece of string (or a skipping rope).

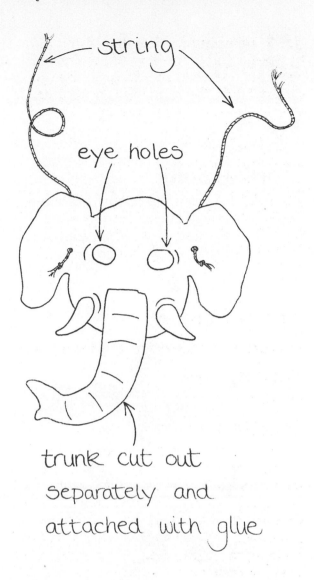

string

eye holes

trunk cut out separately and attached with glue

What to do

Sing the song; and as each elephant comes on to the stage area, he or she should walk along the skipping rope, pretending to balance. A large waving gesture is needed to get the next elephant to come, and the elephants accumulate on the string until there are five elephants on a piece of string. Then everyone shouts 'and it broke' and all the elephants fall on to the floor. They should then pick themselves up and bow before leaving the stage. Encores of this one are always popular and the number of elephants can be extended.

39

If I was not at . . . school

Topics

Ourselves; My town.

Starting point

As always — learn the song! This one is based on a well-known variety song. The children will need to know it really well if they are to sing it with confidence. But if you do not know the tune, it will work just as well as a rhyme.

What you need

You will need the words to the song, modified to suit the classroom context.

Chorus If I was not at . . . school,
[insert your school's name]
Someone else I'd like to be.
If I was not at . . . school,
A *farmer* I would be.
[insert appropriate word]
You'd hear me all day long,
Singing out this song.

Verse 1 Driving tractors, driving tractors, Milking cows all day.
[repeat]

Verse 2 Climbing ladders, climbing ladders,
Hosing down the flames.
*[repeat] *fireman**

Verse 3 Stand on tiptoe, stand on tiptoe, Pirhouette around.
*[repeat] *dancer**

Verse 4 Catch the robbers, catch the robbers,
Throw them into jail.
*[repeat] *policeman**

What to do

Some sort of costume is necessary to match the characters to the verses above, but you can adapt the verses to suit your available costumes or your chosen topic, e.g., for a Mother's Day assembly, a verse on 'A mummy I would be'.

Devise some simple actions for each character to match the words of the song and encourage the children to act out their verse. The song is cumulative, with each verse having the previous ones tagged on the end (a bit like 'Old McDonald had a farm'), so whoever goes first will have to do their bit four times, but whoever goes last will only have to do it once.

Shops and shopping

Chapter four

Most classrooms have a shop at some point during the year. Usually there is a very close link with the maths topic of 'Money' and the shop is introduced with the object of familiarising children with the concepts of exchanging money for goods.

Some schools prefer to use real coins instead of cardboard imitation money. This is a decision which needs to be taken by individual schools and teachers on the basis of their knowledge of their school and class. However, this could prove to be a drain on the pocket if temptation proves too great for the children. We always use plastic tokens in our role-play areas and even they keep disappearing!

The shoe shop

Topics

Big and little; Clothes.

Starting point

One of the highlights of any young child's life is a visit to the shoe shop to buy new shoes. It is a source of great pride to a young child, and children have been known to go to bed in their beautiful new shoes and refuse to take them off! Any class of children will want to talk on this subject and a role-play area which includes cast-off shoes of all kinds will appeal to girls and boys alike.

What you need

All the trappings of a shoe shop: different kinds of shoes (clean) and handbags (jumble sales are a good source of both); display racks, shoeboxes, shoe-trees, a shoe-horn, a foot-measure; a cash register and some money; an unbreakable mirror or mirror tiles placed at floor level; ideally, the kind of small stool used in shoe shops for the assistant to sit on while trying on the customers' shoes — if not, a small pouffe or a footstool will do; tabards and sticky labels if uniforms are required for the sales staff; paper, pens, felt-tipped pens.

What to do

Try to arrange a visit to a shoe shop. If this is not possible, read *Two Shoes, New Shoes* by Shirley Hughes (Walker Books).

Ask the children to decide if the salesperson should wear a uniform. If the decision is 'yes', provide tabards with sticky labels for the children to write their own name badge and stick it on their uniform.

Always provide some form of mark-making equipment, if only a felt-tipped pen to write the prices of the shoes on the boxes.

It will be necessary to provide currency notes if realistic prices are to be charged for the shoes. These can, of course, be bought, but how about letting the children design their own school currency and cheques for use in the shop?

The chip shop

Topics
Food; Ourselves.

Starting point
Talk to your children about the sorts of shops they visit regularly. Depending on the responses you get, ask about their favourite chip-shop foods. Suggest that they might like to have a chip shop as the role-play area for a half-term.

What you need
White coats and hats (old white shirts and paper hats will do), plastic trays, scoops and forks, cartons for peas, rolltop breadbins or other containers for the chips, salt shakers, jars or small bottles for vinegar, yellow sponge cut into strips for chips, thick cardboard cut into fish shapes, pan-scrub (brown) for fish cakes, a cash register and money, paper bags and newspaper for wrapping, card for menus, felt-tipped pens, a telephone, a paper pad and pen for taking orders.

What to do
To give the children a sense of ownership of the chip shop, encourage them to provide the materials and to help set up the role-play corner.

At the risk of repeating it too often, do try to take the children to your local chip shop on a visit first. A packet of chips or two shared out would be a great treat and the children will probably notice much more when they are visiting from school than when they go there with their parents for Friday's tea.

Involve the children in the planning of the shop layout and the menus for display. Provide a telephone and a pad with a pen for taking orders, and encourage organised imaginative play.

The garden centre

Topics
Our town; Growing things.

Starting point
Why not adopt an area of the school grounds and encourage the children to come up with ideas for improving it? A visit to your local garden centre would help them decide what improvements they would like to make, as well as giving them a direct experience to use as a foundation for role-playing.

What you need

Potted plants (preferably made of plastic or paper as real ones would not survive the handling); empty flowerpots, Gro-bags, a selection of gardening tools which the children can handle safely; packets of seeds; bags filled with sand or polystyrene packaging labelled 'Fertiliser'; garden ornaments (if required); a cash register and money; carrier bags; a trolley of some sort.

What to do

Encourage the children to establish a system for the running of the garden centre and to decide on the length of turns and tasks to be performed by the staff. Encourage co-operative play and fair turn-taking. Extend interest by adding a café for shoppers to drop in. Charge realistic prices for produce and provide high-denomination notes so that large purchases can be made.

The newsagent

Topics

Communications; The street.

Starting point

As always, work should start from the experience of the child, so ask your class about the kind of shops they have near their homes. They are likely to mention a 'sweet shop' which probably sells sweets, occasional groceries and newspapers, a bit like the old-style corner shop. Obviously a visit to the nearest shop of this type would be an excellent stimulus, but otherwise a story such as *Wait and See* by Tony Bradman (Little Mammoth) or *The Elephant and the Bad Baby* by Elfrida Vipont and Raymond Briggs (Puffin Picture Books) would introduce the idea that there can be many different kinds of shops.

What you need

Old newspapers, old magazines on specialist topics such as cars, fishing, beauty, etc.; pieces of wood roughly the size of chocolate bars; Fimo clay, Plasticine, icing sugar, large beads. coloured foil, coloured acetate for making sweets; plastic jars, scoops and scales; paper bags and empty chocolate boxes (preferably the kind with a guide to the different centres); a cash register and money; shaped fluorescent cards for 'special offer' signs (these can usually be obtained from wholesalers who supply shops); paper, pencils, crayons, scissors.

What to do

Encourage your class to make their own newspaper and organise its distribution throughout the school.

Sweets can be made in several different ways:
• Use brightly coloured Fimo clay (the sort that is baked in an ordinary oven) to make some liquorice allsorts. Provide the children with some examples of the real thing to copy if you wish.
• Jelly babies can be made out of Plasticine and coated with icing sugar to give an authentic look.
• Beads or similar small items can be wrapped in different colours of acetate or foil to give a good immitation of chocolates.

Obviously, all the children who use the role-play corner need to be warned very strongly about not putting the pretend sweets in their mouths.

It is also fun for the children to design their own chocolate-bar wrapper to wrap around a wooden block and then sell in the shop. Older children can try to produce several wrappers which are identical, to give the effect of mass-produced chocolate bars. Birthday cards (and the envelopes to fit them) can be another item of stock which the children can design themselves. The choosing,

buying and sending of birthday cards is a good incentive to get the children to change their roles with a good grace.

Encourage the children to use environmental print to advertise their shop and its products. Provide card, pens and the opportunity to put up special offer notices of the children's own devising.

Ensure that the children take turns as customers and shopkeepers.

The toy shop

Topics

Leisure; Young and old.

Starting point

This is a good subject for the role-play corner in the weeks leading up to Christmas, when the children are thinking about what Father Christmas will bring them on Christmas morning. Most children will have no difficulty discussing the sorts of toys found in a toy shop and their own current favourite toy. Most will be visiting toy shops at this time, so they will have the first-hand experience to call upon when discussing the topic. Children in the class who do not celebrate Christmas will still enjoy playing at shopping.

What you need

Toys! Cuddly toys, dolls, construction sets (can be empty boxes), etc. A jumble sale is an excellent source of odds and ends of toys good enough for role-play, such as incomplete jigsaws which can be wrapped and sold as new; a cash register and some money; toy catalogues for ordering; order pads and pencils for filling in orders and prices; wrapping paper, carrier bags.

Ask your class to bring in some old toys of their own which they no longer play with. Provide a section of books for sale.

What to do

Ensure that there is a play area in the shop for the children to play with their toys before deciding on their purchase. A small browsing area for books is essential, with comfortable seating for the 'parents' to come with their 'children'. Encourage careful choosing and ordering. Provide some wrapped parcels which can do flexible duty as any toy ordered by the customer.

The boutique

Topics

Clothes; Hot and cold.

Starting point

As always, the starting points are the children and their experiences. You can also read *Red is Best* by Kathy Stinson (Oxford University Press) and encourage the children to talk about their favourite clothes. Why do they like them? Is it their colour, comfort or is it because they are fashionable?

What you need

Lots of clothes — jumble sales can be an excellent source. Try to include party dresses, sportswear, swimsuits, cloaks, aprons, hats, jewellery, nightwear and various shoes, including football boots. A rail and some hangers are essential and you should have a full-length unbreakable mirror such as the one made by Galt. A changing room with a curtain, however rudimentary, adds to the realism. Card, felt-tipped pens, string and scissors will be useful for making price tags. You will also need a cash register, money and carrier bags.

What to do

Ensure that all the clothes are clean and that there are enough hangers for them to be stored neatly when not in use. Encourage the children to write price tags for each article and attach them to the clothes in some way. Designing a tag and then deciding how to attach it can be a good problem-solving activity.

Agree on rules such as 'only one person at a time in the changing room,

please' and encourage the children to design other notices for other areas of the shop.

The baker's shop

Topics

Harvest; Healthy eating.

Starting point

A baking lesson can be a good start for this role-play. Ask about the children's favourite cakes, bread, pies, etc., and where they come from. Discuss how a baker would make enough bread and cakes to fill the shop. A visit to a local bakery would be ideal, but if this is not possible, read the story of the Little Red Hen (the Margot Zemach edition published by Hutchinson is available in most school libraries). It is a moral tale which also describes what has to be done to make a loaf of bread or a cake.

What you need

White coats and caps (old white shirts and paper hats will do); a choice of materials to make bread, cakes, etc. — plastic foam, wood, cork, polystyrene, egg-boxes, coloured paper, coloured acetate, paper plates, card, pictures of pizza, glue, scissors; a cash register and money; paper bags, cake boxes (these could be designed by the children); paper, pens, pencils.

What to do

Encourage the children to make a large selection of goods for the shop — different types of bread, decorated cakes of various sizes, pies. Cakes can be made from circles of yellow foam, decorated with coloured paper or acetate. Pieces of polystyrene can be decorated with brown paper to look like chocolate meringues. A pizza is easily made by sticking coloured paper onto a circle of card, or even by cutting out a picture of a pizza and sticking it on a paper plate.

Remind the children to keep the shop area clean and tidy, since food kept in a dirty shop would make people ill. This is an excellent opportunity for a lesson on some basic facts of hygiene.

As in every role-play area, full use should be made of opportunities to use environmental writing in the form of messages, notes, orders, notices, lists, etc.

Drama through rhymes

Chapter five

Children love rhymes, especially funny ones, and will often spontaneously improvise actions to match the words. This dramatic expression within a familiar framework also gives the sense of security which is so important for the development of confidence in young children.

It is always far easier to recite a rhyme in chorus, and some of the more timid children may never wish to do more than this. Solo speakers should always be volunteers!

Ten little Christmas trees

Starting point

I have always found this rhyme useful at Christmas during storytime, but it can also be used as a simple early-years contribution to a whole-school production or as a small part of a traditional nativity play, before the actual play starts.

What you need

The words of the following rhyme, Christmas-tree costumes (see illustration), twenty children.

Green conical paper hat

Green material circle with hole for head

Ten little Christmas trees standing in a line,
One went to X's house and then there were nine.
Nine little Christmas trees, standing very straight,
One went to X's house and then there were eight.
Eight little Christmas trees said 'Christmas will be heaven',
One went to X's house, and then there were seven.
Seven little Christmas trees, all as straight as sticks,
One went to X's house, and then there were six.
Six little Christmas trees, growing and alive,
One went to X's house, and then there were five.
Five little Christmas trees said, 'Will they want some more?'
One went to X's house, and then there were four.
Four little Christmas trees, giggling with glee,
One went to X's house, and then there were three.
Three little Christmas trees, with nothing much to do,
One went to X's house, and then there were two.
Two little Christmas trees, having lots of fun,
One went to X's house, and then there was one.
One little Christmas tree, feeling very small,
He/she came to our school and that was best of all!

What to do

Either read the poem yourself (this is quickest and easiest, but not necessarily best, approach) or ask some children from your own or an older class to read it.

The two sets of ten children should stand apart from each other if possible and as each of the children to be named goes to claim his or her tree, they could stand holding hands at the centre of the stage.

'Christmas trees' should hold their hands out to the sides to make the traditional shape. Part of the usefulness of this poem is that half the cast just need to wear their usual school clothes!

In a dark, dark wood

Topics
Light and dark; Magic and mystery.

Starting point
A version of this traditional rhyme can be found in *A Dark, Dark Tale* by Ruth Brown (Red Fox). Some children may find this poem frightening, so introduce it at storytime first and let everyone learn it by heart. This seems to change the scary element into fun.

What you need
The words of the following poem:

> In a dark, dark wood, there was a dark, date gate.
> And through the dark, dark gate there was a dark, dark path.
> And up the dark, dark path there was a dark, dark house.
> And in the dark, dark house there was a dark, dark door.
> And through the dark, dark door there was a dark, dark hall.
> And in the dark, dark hall there was a dark, dark stair.
> And up the dark, dark stair there was a dark, dark room.
> And in the dark, dark room there was a dark, dark cupboard.
> And in the dark, dark cupboard there was a dark, dark box.
> And in the dark, dark box there was a . . . GHOST!

You will also need musical instruments for sound effects and pictures, preferably children's paintings, of the items in the poem. These should be mounted on cardboard for durability in rehearsals.

What to do
Stand one set of eleven children who are taking part in a line across the front of the stage. Allocate a musical instrument to each of the eleven children in the other set, one instrument for each object in the poem, as in the following example.

> In a dark, dark wood,
> [Guiro]
> There was a dark, dark gate.
> [Swannee whistle]
> And through the dark, dark gate,
> [Swannee whistle again]
> There was a dark, dark path.
> [marracas]

Speakers need to practise leaving a pause after each object is mentioned in order to fit in the sound effects.

Children holding the pictures need not also say the poem, in which case you will need either one soloist or a choral group. It is very effective to start off with one child speaking for the first item and have another child join in for each new item, thus getting louder and louder as the end approaches.

The picture-holders should stand with their backs to the audience to start with and as each item is mentioned for the first time, the child holding the right picture turns round to show it to the audience. At the last verse, everyone shouts 'GHOST!' and all the instruments play together for one beat. Then there should be silence.

Little Miss Muffet

Topics
Hot and cold; Minibeasts.

Starting point
Recite the rhyme 'Little Miss Muffet'. Hopefully, the children will know it and will say it with you. If not, spend some time at storytime teaching it. This is a quick and easy piece of role-play which works well with nursery children.

Little Miss Muffet
Sat on a tuffet,
Eating her curds and whey;
There came a big spider,
Who sat down beside her
And frightened Miss Muffet away.

What you need
An unbreakable plastic bowl and a spoon for Miss Muffet, a large cardboard

cut-out of a spider, either on its own, attached to a tabard, or stuck on to a hat.

What to do
Ask for two volunteers to be the spider and Miss Muffet, then simply recite the rhyme and let the two act out their parts. This is an everyday bit of drama which the children never seem to tire of and it is so easy that everyone can have a go.

Here's a banana for Tommy to eat

Topics
Transport; Harvest.

Starting point
As always, help the children to learn the poem so that they will feel comfortable saying it in front of an audience.

What you need
You will need costumes (or at least hats) for all the characters in the rhyme. The child just needs to be dressed in ordinary school clothes. Mum can wear a headscarf and carry a basket — or it can be Dad if you prefer! All the characters can be of either sex. You should also have an apron for the greengrocer, a bobble hat for the van driver, a boiler suit and a baseball cap for the train driver, a peaked cap for the captain, goggles and a flying helmet for the pilot and a straw hat for the farmer. And do not forget a real or plastic banana.

Here's a banana for Tommy to eat
> [insert the name of the child who is to play the part]

Here is the mother who's shopping for tea,
Who buys the banana for Tommy to eat.

Here's the greengrocer called Mr(s) McGhee,
Who chats to the mother who's shopping for tea
To buy the banana for Tommy to eat.

Here's the van driver who follows his route
Straight to the greengrocer, etc.

Here's the train driver whose train goes toot-toot,
Who meets the van driver who follows his route, etc.

Here's the ship's captain delivering fruit,
Who knows the train driver whose train goes toot-toot, etc.

Here's the air pilot who flies to the docks,
To meet the ship's captain delivering fruit, etc.

Here's the poor farmer who works where it's hot,
To harvest bananas before they can rot,
Who sells to the pilot who flies to the docks, etc.

When the whole poem has reached the child again, he or she should step forward and say, 'But I don't like bananas!'

What to do
Ask the children to recite the poem while the 'principals' step forward in turn and pass the banana along the line.

It is possible and amusing to have some sound effects at the back of the group. A BBC sound-effects record can be taped in individual parts so that each time the aeroplane, boat, van or train are mentioned, the sound is there to match. It is best to have four children with four tape-recorders, each having a continuous sound, each to be switched on and off when the appropriate part of the poem is being spoken.

The house that Jack built

Topics
Houses; Materials.

Starting point
Read the rhyme to your class several times. Some of the children may know it and will join in, especially with the ending phrase.

This is the house that Jack built.

This is the malt
That lay in the house
that Jack built.

This is the rat,
That ate the malt
That lay in the house
that Jack built.

This is the cat,
That killed the rat,
That ate the malt
Thay lay in the house
that Jack built.

This is the dog,
That worried the cat,
That killed the rat,
That ate the malt
That lay in the house
that Jack built.

This is the cow with the crumpled horn,
That tossed the dog,
That worried the cat,
That killed the rat,
That ate the malt
That lay in the house
that Jack built.

This is the maiden all forlorn,
That milked the cow with the crumpled horn,
That tossed the dog,
That worried the cat,

That killed the rat,
That ate the malt
That lay in the house
that Jack built.

This is the man all tattered and torn,
That kissed the maiden all forlorn,
That milked the cow with the crumpled
    horn,
That tossed the dog,
That worried the cat,
That killed the rat,
That ate the malt
That lay in the house
that Jack built.

This is the priest all shaven and shorn,
That married the man all tattered and
    torn,
That kissed the maiden all forlorn,
That milked the cow with the crumpled
    horn,
That tossed the dog,
That worried the cat,
That killed the rat,
That ate the malt
Thay lay in the house
that Jack built.

This is the cock that crowed in the morn,
That waked the priest all shaven and
    shorn,
That married the man all tattered and
    torn,
That kissed the maiden all forlorn,
That milked the cow with the crumpled
    horn,
That tossed the dog,
That worried the cat,
That killed the rat,
That ate the malt
Thay lay in the house
that Jack built.

What you need

You will need the following costumes for
the different characters: Jack can wear
overalls and carry a building tool such as
a trowel. Bags or sacks of any sort
labelled 'Malt' can be used. The rat, the

cat, the dog and the cow can all wear
headbands with the appropriate shape
of ears (see illustration on page 15). If a
full costume is required, leotards and
footless tights or polo-necked sweaters
and tights in black, grey and brown make
very successful animal costumes.
For the cow, two children in a painted
sheet with a child at the front wearing a
headdress will greatly amuse the
audience. The maiden can wear a mob-
cap and carry a bucket. The man all
tattered and torn needs jagged edges to
his trousers and holes in his jacket. Bare
feet could be appropriate, while a top
hat is essential. The priest can wear either
a dog collar (a modern version) or a
dark dressing gown with a cord around
the waist (skipping rope will do) and a
paper 'tonsure' on his/her head held in
place with sticky tape or a hairgrip and
removed very carefully. The cockerel
needs a headband with a beak (see
illustration on page 16).

The house can be a flat painting mounted on cardboard or a large cardboard box made to look like a house – preferably, of course, made by the children as part of the class work on technology.

What to do

This rhyme works well at a class assembly, when treated as choral verse-speaking. The teacher can 'conduct' the chorus, giving them signs to start and stop. For instance, there should always be a slight pause after the introduction of each new character:

'This is the maiden all forlorn/[pause] Who milked the cow with a crumpled horn', etc. During this pause, the maiden curtseys. She also curtseys every subsequent time she is mentioned. All the other characters have a piece of 'business' each, too: The cockerel shouts 'Cock-a-doodledoo'; the man raises his hat; the cow moos and bows (both ends!); the dog barks; the cat miaouws; the rat nibbles at something imaginary in its paws; Jack gestures towards his house.

If children in your class are too young to learn to recite this rhyme, you can, of course, read it yourself or ask a group of older children from another class to do it for you.

Billy Brown and friends

Topics

Ourselves; Feelings.

Starting point

There is always a place in the nursery or infant classroom for short rhymes which the children learn by heart and love to say for the sound patterns they make.

They are easy to join in and immediately suggest actions to go with them. This sort of rhyme is the very earliest form of dramatic performance and should happen every day in every classroom. Young children need lots of it!

What you need

A rhyme such as the following one and a relaxed environment, probably storytime at the end of the day.

> Billy Brown had a frown. Can you
> frown like Billy Brown?
> Chrissie Crimper had a simper. Can
> you simper like Chrissie Crimper?
> Milly Miff had a sniff. Can you sniff like
> Milly Miff?
> Hetty Hulk had a sulk. Can you sulk like
> Hetty Hulk?
> But Lucy Lyle had the brightest smile.
> Can you smile like Lucy Lyle?

You will also need some unbreakable mirrors.

What to do

Read the rhyme to the children, explaining any words such as 'simper' and demonstrating the sort of facial expression each word conveys. Encourage them to join in with verbal expressions to match the facial expressions. You could pass some unbreakable mirrors around the group while they are saying the poem, so that they can see if their faces are doing what they think they are doing!

We're going on a bear hunt

Topics

Animals; Feelings.

Starting point

Talk to your class about what 'hunting' means — you could play 'hunt-the-thimble' to illustrate. You may also want to read to your class *Bear Hunt* by Anthony Browne (Hippo Books).

What you need

For a storytime session, you will just need yourself and your class. If it is to be a performance for an audience, you will need to divide your class into two groups, one acting as an 'echo' of the other.

CHORUS 1

First group	**Second group**
We're going on a bear hunt,	We're going on a bear hunt,
We're going to catch a big one,	We're going to catch a big one,
We're not scared!	We're not scared!

Both

Verse 1
Uuuugh! Grass! Long, tickly grass right up to our necks!

CHORUS 2

First group	**Second group**
Can't go under it,	Can't go under it,
Can't go over it,	Can't go over it,
Can't go around it.	Can't go around it.

Both
Oh no! We've got to go through it!
(Swish, swish, swish, swish)

This basic structure repeats itself, with only the verse and the sound of the obstacle changing:

Verse 2
Yuk! Rocks! Hard rocks that hurt your feet!

(Chorus then says, 'Can't fly over them!')
(Bang, bang, bang, bang)

Verse 3
Aaaargh! Mud! Thick, sticky mud right up to our knees!
(Slurp, slurp, slurp, slurp)

Verse 4
Oooooh! A river! A wide, flowing river as deep as can be!
(Splash, splash, splash, splash)

Verse 5
Whoops! A cave! A dark cave in the rock!
(Tiptoe, tiptoe, tiptoe, tiptoe)

First group	**Second group**
I can feel something,	I can feel something,
I think it's got claws,	Yes, it's got claws,
I think it's got fur,	Yes, it's got fur,
I think it's got teeth.	Yes, it's got teeth.

Both
Oh no! We've found a bear!

First group	**Second group**
Back across the river!	(Splash, splash, splash, splash)
Through the sticky mud!	(Slurp, slurp, slurp, slurp)
Through the hard rocks!	(Bang, bang, bang, bang)
Through the long grass!	(Swish, swish, swish, swish)
And home!	(Phew, thank goodness for that!)

CHORUS 3

First group	**Second group**
We've been on a bear hunt,	We've been on a bear hunt,
We really found a big one,	We really found a big one,
We weren't scared. [pause]	We weren't scared.

Single voice
Oh yes, we were!

What to do
Encourage the children to think of actions to fit each of the different obstacles, e.g., pushing aside the long grass or making hands behave as feet would in deep sticky mud. Actions are also a good idea for Chorus 2, with hands held high, low and then circled to suggest 'around'. On 'Oh no!', they can clutch their fists to their heads as if in despair.

Since this performance needs no costumes, it is a simple activity which is great fun to do. Of course, if you say the rhyme at intervals throughout the year with your class, you will be ready for a performance whenever it is needed.

Places of interest

Chapter six

In most places of interest, children are very much the passive accompaniments to their parents and other adults who do all the important and interesting things, while the children are told to wait quietly and not to touch.

In this chapter, therefore, there are suggestions for role-play areas which give the control over to children and enable them to imitate adult behaviour as they see it.

The camp site

Topics
Holidays; Houses and homes.

Starting point
Discuss with the class the reasons why people go camping. Is it because it is more fun? Cheaper than staying at a hotel? Healthier? Easier to move from place to place? Hopefully, some of the children will have been on a camping holiday of some kind or else to a Cub or Brownie camp.

What you need
Borrow or make at least two small tents which can be put up without knocking holes in the floor. A firmly anchored piece of rope with a sheet over it is perfectly acceptable.

You could, of course, pitch your tents on the grass if you have any in the school grounds. The only problem with this is the security aspect – if you cannot leave them out overnight, it is a nuisance to have to keep bringing them indoors. You will also need an imitation camp-fire (red acetate and logs), sleeping bags, a camp stove (no gas cylinder though), a folding table and some chairs, packets and tins of food, plastic cutlery and crockery (a picnic basket is useful), tricycles, shorts and T-shirts, large sheets of paper or an old sheet, paint, paintbrushes.

What to do
Talk about camping and decide where the majority of the class would prefer to stay, either at a site by the seaside or in the country. The children can then design and paint a suitable scene as a backdrop for their camp site. Encourage them to organise the site so that it is always clean and tidy, since rubbish left lying around would cause germs to breed and would make the campers ill.

The zoo

Topics

Animals; Conservation.

Starting point

Read the story *Dear Zoo* by Rod Campbell (Picture Puffin) and talk about the reasons why the child in the story could not keep the animals sent by the zoo. The best way to develop this theme would, of course, be to go on a visit to a real zoo. If this is not possible, you could make do with singing songs such as 'Going to the Zoo' and saying poems and rhymes about various zoo animals.

What you need

Lots of (borrowed) cuddly toys of the various animals found in zoos and/or models of animals made from papier mâché; large cardboard boxes to make stalls or skipping ropes to rope off areas for the animals; uniforms for the zoo staff, stethoscope and white coat for the vet; buckets of animal feed; card and felt-tipped pens to make notices, tickets, a cash register and money; squared paper, pencils (optional).

What to do

Encourage the children in your class to design the layout of the zoo on squared paper cut to the size of the actual role-play area. They need to consider which animals can go next to each other. Would the deer be happy next to the lions?

The visitors will have to buy tickets and the zoo keeper can show them round, allowing them to stroke the animals which are tame.

Animals need to be fed and cleaned if they are to remain healthy, and there should be zoo staff with this responsibility for each of the animals. Of course, lots of signs will need to be made for the zoo; for example, 'This way to the lions' and 'Please do not feed the penguins'.

If your children become really fascinated by their zoo, they can develop it further, for instance, by providing a snack bar or a gift shop for visitors.

A very similar approach can be used to create your own farm in the role-play area.

The airport

Topics
Transport; Leisure.

Starting point
Most children have been on an aeroplane these days, or else they have seen it on television or heard about it from friends.

This is a good role-play area either for the summer term leading up to the holidays or for the first weeks back at school, when memories of holidays are still fresh.

What you need
Pairs of chairs with an aisle between them, next to a wall; a kiosk or tables for customs, passport control and ticket barriers; luggage of various kinds (from jumble sales); pilot's cap, cabin crew uniforms (scarf and hat for the stewardess, waistcoat and bow tie for the steward); a large outline of an aeroplane on the wall (see illustration) behind the chairs; two pairs of headphones for the pilot and co-pilot; kitchen area (from home-corner?) at the back; paper, card, pens, felt-tipped pens, scissors and glue to make passports and tickets.

What to do
Place the chairs as in the illustration below. Discuss with the children which destinations they want to fly to.

The children might want to design and make their own tickets and passports. They could also decide on menus and whether there is going to be a first- and a second-class cabin.

They will then need to decide who will be the pilot, the customs officer, the passport controller, the porter, etc.

The baby clinic

Topics
Ourselves; Big and little.

Starting point
If one of the children in the class has had a new baby at home recently, mother and baby could be invited to school for a visit. Perhaps the baby could be bathed during the visit as this opens up discussion about weighing and feeding, and all the many things a baby needs.

What you need
Baby dolls and dolls' clothes; scales large enough to weigh the largest doll; a baby bath and/or a sink; a table and chairs for waiting parents; buggies; empty baby food containers and plastic baby bottles; nurse's uniforms or blue overalls; a stethoscope and a syringe (Fisher Price doctor's set is recommended for durability); a telephone, a paper pad and pencils; sugar paper, card and felt-tipped pens for making signs and notices; publicity material for baby products.

What to do
Make sure that fathers, as well as mothers, bring in babies to be seen by the staff. Encourage boys to play nurses and girls to be doctors.

Encourage the children to make appointments for the clinic and to put plenty of signs up on the walls. I have always found that drawing outlines on sugar paper for storage of the role-play materials helps the children to put them away properly by themselves, and also draws attention to any items which have been mislaid.

The fair

Topics
Leisure; Light and colour.

Starting point
This is a particularly good role-play theme for a school which has a large number of Travellers' children in the school population, since they often know a great deal about fairs and can display their knowledge.

If you have a fair in your area, a visit to the site during the day should not be too difficult to arrange.

What you need
Simple games such as hoop-la, roll-a-ball (ping-pong balls are excellent), roll-a-coin, knock-down-the-cans (use baby milk cans and bean bags); a cash register, money and tickets; card, paper, coloured paper, cotton wool, coloured cotton wool balls, wooden lolly sticks, discarded popcorn containers, paint, crayons, glue, scissors.

What to do
Encourage the children to design and make the sort of foods found for sale at the fair, for example, candyfloss (pink cotton wool on lolly sticks), lollipops (decorated cardboard circles on sticks), ice-cream (cardboard cones with cotton wool balls of different colours glued to them).

Decisions have to be made about winning scores and prizes for the winners at the stalls. Do they get money back or a small prize? Posters describing the prizes can then be made and displayed throughout the school. Posters for each of the attractions should also be designed and displayed prominently to draw in the customers.

Outer space

Topics
Space travel; Transport.

Starting point
This is one area where a visit is not an option, unless it is to a science centre which has a space theme.

I have found that a set of Space LEGO makes a good starting point as some of the children create whole landscapes to go with their constructions. Any television coverage of the current space programme can be recorded for school use.

What you need
Follow the 'outline' approach used for the aeroplane on page 62 or use a large cardboard box, decorated to look like a rocket (the children should decorate it themselves). For spacesuits, you can use tabards made of any metallic fabric — a silver lamé evening dress found at a jumble sale could make two tabards. These can be topped with silver card headbands decorated with sequins. Alternatively, children could make space helmets from cuboid cardboard boxes covered in aluminium foil, with a face-plate cut out in front. Foil-covered wellingtons make good moon boots. For realistic oxygen tanks,

two plastic lemonade bottles can be wrapped together with insulating tape, then sprayed with metallic paint or covered in foil. (Any spraying has to be done by an adult in a well-ventilated room, or closely supervised.) Attach elastic for shoulder straps.

For a suitable background, provide lots of black paper and adhesive stars in various sizes. Pictures of planets and rockets might also be fun, so provide paper, paint and brushes for the children to paint these.

What to do

Involve the children in the design and making of their lunar landscape. Black paper with silver stars will do the job on its own, but children's paintings of rockets and space stations will look far brighter and more interesting. There will have to be a limit on the number of astronauts in the rocket if it is not to disintegrate very quickly. You will also need astronauts to staff the mission control and decide on the course to take, so there are plenty of interesting roles to consider.

Puppets galore

Chapter seven

Puppets are the ideal medium for developing the language of children who have problems with their speech, are shy and withdrawn, speak English as a second language or indeed, as in the case of some children, have to cope with all three of these challenges.

A puppet enables a child to pretend to be another character and to discard his or her everyday personality. This is especially useful when children are encouraged to use their puppets for free play in the role-play area. Without a continual adult presence, shy children may come out of their shells and venture to express themselves through the voice of the puppet.

There are hundreds of uses to which puppets can be put in drama and role-play. The following suggestions are interchangeable and I have not suggested any topics, since they can be applied to any topic.

Paper-bag puppets

Starting point

Read a story with two main characters who speak to each other a lot. I have always found *The Princess and the Frog* excellent for this but you could use a modern story instead, for example *Bet You Can't* by Penny Dale (Walker Books) or *Little Bear* by Else Holmelund Minarik (Mammoth).

What you need

Paper bags big enough to fit easily on to a child's hand but not too big to fall off all the time; crayons, felt-tipped pens; an adhesive stick; sequins, wool, scraps of fabric and other collage materials; a cassette recorder with a microphone and a blank cassette.

What to do

Ask the children to draw faces of the two main characters in the story on the paper bags. They can then put one on each hand so that the two characters can 'talk'

to one another. Encourage the children to retell the story by putting appropriate words into their puppets' mouths. Split the class into groups and let the children work with the tape recorder until they have a dialogue which they feel is satisfactory. When everyone has had a go, play it back during a get-together time and ask the children to tell you which hand is 'speaking' — the princess or the frog. If anyone is not satisfied with their taped dialogue, try to provide time for them to record it again. In a nursery or reception class this could be an ongoing activity set up in a corner for the children to return to at will.

This activity is also very useful with Year 2 children to help them distinguish between a play, where the words express the action, and a story, where the words describe the action. Plays written by individual children or by groups are also an excellent subject for critical re-drafting. Different groups of children could write different scenes and the resulting play could be performed during the class assembly or for the whole school.

Wooden-spoon puppets

Starting point

These puppets can be used to depict any simple story. The Nativity story can be effectively performed in this way, as can 'Cinderella' and 'Hansel and Gretel'.

What you need

Cheap wooden spoons from a cut-price store — size is unimportant, so sets of three different sizes are fine; collage materials suitable for the story you are working on. You will need lots of wool or fur in colours suitable for hair. You may find it best to pre-cut fabric into rectangles the depth of the spoon handles and allow children to choose from these; adhesive, scissors, felt-tipped pens, elastic bands.

What to do

Let the children decide which character their puppet is to be and encourage them to dress it accordingly. They should then draw a suitable face on the back of the spoon. Fabric should be gathered into the 'neck' of the spoon with an elastic band to make the puppet's clothing (see illustration).

The puppets can be made to 'perform' behind a low storage trolley for trays, if no other form of stage is available. You may find it best to split your class up into groups to decide on their version of the story. If everybody decides to make a puppet of the main character, there will have to be some tactful suggestions that they pretend it is another character, just for the performance.

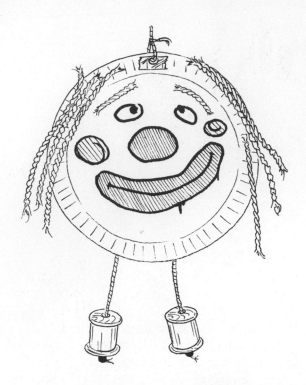

Paper-plate puppets

Starting point

Talk about the shape of a paper plate with your class. Could it be used for other things besides eating food from it? If you drew on it with felt-tipped pens, what could you turn it into? Hold the plate in front of your face and demonstrate how it could be used to make another face — a mask — to pretend to be someone else.

What you need

Paper plates, felt-tipped pens, collage materials, string, bobbins, egg-boxes, sticks, sticky tape, adhesive, scissors, a hole punch, a cassette recorder and tapes of dance music.

What to do

Remind the children that the plate is already making the round shape of a face and that their job is to draw in the eyes, nose and mouth.

Let the children work in groups to create faces for themselves. Some may be content to draw, others may want to paint their puppet green or stick on some wool for hair. Do stress that the puppet should be someone that the children would like to pretend to be, not necessarily just the same as their friend's.

There are two types of puppets the children can make:
1. Attach a stick to the back of the plate, using sticky tape, so that the plate can be held in front of a child's face. Cut out eyeholes (you may need to do this for the children).
2. Using two bobbins and string, make dangling feet for the puppet (see illustration). You may need to tie a knot at each end of the piece of string. Attach the 'legs' to the back of the plate with a piece of sticky tape. Tie another piece of string to the top of the plate, preferably through a hole reinforced with sticky tape.

Play some dance music and encourage the children to make their puppets dance to it, to start off free play.

Cotton-wool caterpillars

Starting point

This is a useful puppet to make in early summer, when the real caterpillars are available for inspection. Ask the children to look at some caterpillars through a magnifying glass and talk about their shape and movement.

What you need

Lots of cotton-wool balls — these can be white or various pastel colours (pale green is particularly useful); sturdy thread (Sylko Perle is an ideal strength for this

activity); blunt-ended large needles or bodkins; white self-adhesive label 'spots'; felt-tipped pens, finger paint, paint, paintbrushes, scissors, adhesive.

What to do

Decide in advance what length your caterpillar is going to be. Six cotton-wool balls are usually adequate, although seven or eight allow more movement.

Thread the needle with the thread (encourage the children to try doing it themselves) and show them how to push the needle through the cotton-wool balls to make their caterpillar. A large knot or a bead on the end will prevent the balls falling off.

Mix paint with PVA adhesive for the children to paint their caterpillar in stripes and spots. Finger paint could also be used to dab spots on the cotton wool. Do not let the caterpillars get soggy or they will fall to pieces! When the caterpillars are dry, the children can colour the white self-adhesive dots black to make eyes for their caterpillars.

The caterpillar is now ready to be played with, but remind the children that it will not stand up to much rough usage. Rhymes such as 'Little Arabella Miller' and Spike Milligan's 'I Wish I Was a Caterpillar' can be used effectively with this puppet.

A similar puppet can be made from large macaroni theaded on a piece of string. A large bead or other object slightly larger than the hole in the pasta must be put on the string first and secured in place with a knot. Stick a forked tongue on the end and you have a wiggly snake. The pasta can be dyed in advance in a pot of concentrated food colouring (for example, green and yellow pieces to be used alternately). This makes a really colourful snake which needs no extra painting. Children should be involved in choosing the colours and dyeing the pasta.

Stick puppets

Starting point

Explain to the children that they are going to make a puppet from one of their own drawings or paintings.

What you need

Sheets of thin, flexible card, felt-tipped pens, scissors, paper fasteners, sticks for the puppets, sticky tape.

What to do

Ask the children to draw the person they want their puppet to be on thin card. Stress that their pictures should have arms and legs as these are going to move. Provide a thin black felt-tipped pen for

paper fastener

stick

drawing the outline of the puppet to help the children cut it out. Once the figure has been completed to the child's satisfaction, it should then be cut out, preferably by the child; but if this would mean no puppet because it had accidentally been hacked to pieces in an attempt to cut it out, by all means give some assistance.

The legs (and arms, if possible) need to be cut off and loosely joined back to the torso using paper fasteners. The stick can then be attached to the torso with sticky tape to make a jointed stick puppet (see illustration). These puppets can then be used for a performance, in which each child in turn says something about their character. This is very effective for a Mother's Day assembly, especially if the puppeteers are hidden behind a curtain and the audience has to guess the identities of the speakers.

Stick puppets can also be used as shadow puppets if a white sheet and a strong source of light are available.

Paper-cup puppets

Starting point

Make two paper-cup puppets to illustrate a song or a rhyme you often tell to your class. Around Christmas time, it could be 'Two little dicky-birds' with the cups decorated to look like robins. In the spring you could have two blue-tits.

What you need

Paper cups (<u>not</u> plastic), small pieces of yellow card for beaks, paint mixed with a small amount of PVA adhesive, feathers for tails, felt-tipped pens, gummed paper, short sticks or pieces of cane, white adhesive dots for eyes, scissors, adhesive, sticky tape.

yellow card beak

white adhesive dot, eye drawn with felt-tipped pen

red gummed paper

brown gummed paper

feather

stick fastened inside cup

What to do

After saying your chosen rhyme using your puppets for the actions, invite the children to make puppets of their own, either to illustrate the same rhyme or some other rhyme.

Display the puppets in the book corner so that everyone can 'have a go' with all the puppets.

Make-believe places

Chapter eight

Magic and fantasy have always been a part of our lives. Whether as adults or as children, we have used our imagination to create different surroundings for ourselves, imaginary friends, imaginary fame and fortune. In books, television and films many impossible worlds are presented in a lifelike way, often in a cartoon form. Children bring these images to school with them and enjoy the chance to join their heroes, and forget about the everyday world around them by pretending that make-believe is real.

A rainbow-coloured Christmas

Topics
Colours; Toys; Celebrations.

Starting point
Talk about the different colours and where they occur in nature and in man-made objects. You could read – or ask the children to read – *Red is Best* by Kathy Stinson (OUP), in which a little girl describes how red clothes make her feel happiest.

What you need
Tabards or other costumes in each of the colours you decide to use; a fairy costume – this could be a tutu or an angel costume decorated with ribbons and tinsel (either will need a wand); a child-sized Father Christmas costume; Christmas presents to match the chosen colours, for example, a red dress, a green bicycle, black shoes. One of these should be painted all the colours of the rainbow – alternatively, you could wrap it in multicoloured ribbons; a white backcloth; an overhead projector with sheets of coloured acetate; a glockenspiel to announce the entrance of the Christmas Fairy; a cassette recorder and tapes of music to express the different colours, for example, 'Morning' from *Peer Gynt* by E. Grieg for green and 'Mars' from *The Planets* by G. Holst for red.

What to do
With the three-year-old nursery children, it would be unrealistic to aim for a stage performance. Instead, you could ask older children to come and talk to the nursery children individually about their favourite colours. The older children could then go back to their classroom and write a short account of what they said. These could then be read aloud in the nursery classroom, while the children just hold up their coloured objects. With older children, the teacher or another adult can act as the narrator.

Devise a scene where a group of children talk about what they would like for Christmas, for example, a green shirt or a yellow hat. One child cannot decide on the colour of her present (whatever it is that you decided would be your multicoloured object), and wishes someone else helped her decide.

The wish is answered by the Christmas Fairy (glockenspiel should be struck whenever she appears on stage), who offers to show the children all the different colours in the Land of the Rainbow.

The fairy and the children together 'visit' the different colours, each of which explains why they are 'the best'. Any appropriate songs can also be sung.

In the end, the indecisive child chooses all the colours of the rainbow, rather than just one.

The performance ends with Father Christmas bringing presents to the sleeping children. They wake up on Christmas morning with their presents around them.

After the performance, remember to put the costumes in the role-play area, so that the children can stage their own version.

Father Christmas's workshop

Topics
Toys; Celebrations.

Starting point
This production could develop out of the topic of 'Toys'. Any book on toys coming to life such as the *Old Bear* series by Jane Hissey would make a good topic for class dicussion.

What you need
A Father Christmas costume to fit a child; children's pyjamas; elf costumes — belted tabards with gold cardboard buckles, pointed hats, tights, felt slippers with pointed toes (optional), felt or crêpe-paper neck- and wrist frills (see illustration); costumes for toys — frilly dresses for dolls, beige/brown polo necks and tights, and masks (or headbands with ears) for teddy bears; large cardboard jigsaw shapes to hang around the necks of the children in the Jigsaw Land; large cardboard outlines of books to be worn by children in the Book Land; Christmas

wrapping paper; wrapped-up boxes full of children's toys; sacks for the elves; piano music or a cassette recorder and tapes of the appropriate songs.

What to do

In the opening scene, it is Christmas Eve in Father Christmas's workshop. Suddenly one of the elves rushes in and announces that all the toys have been stolen, so there will be no Christmas presents for children in the whole world. Father Christmas then says that he will go to the Toy Land to get some more. Accompanied by elves, Father Christmas visits the Teddy Bear Land, the Jigsaw Land, the Doll Land and the Book Land. In each part of Toy Land, the toys greet him with a song and/or a short dance, and present him with boxed toys, which the elves put in their sacks. Songs for the

toys might include 'Doll on a music box' (from *Chitty Chitty Bang Bang*) and 'Teddy Bears' picnic'; you should also ask the children for their own suggestions.

In the next scene, Father Christmas and the elves are busy wrapping presents and putting them in the sacks. In the last scene, a group of children in pyjamas wake up on the Christmas morning and open their presents. Father Christmas, the elves and the toys from the Toy Land come on stage, and they all sing 'We wish you a merry Christmas'.

It is important to start the production with only the basic story outline and to encourage the children to improvise dialogue, which then becomes more memorable for the children. You could also take advantage of any natural comic talents in the classroom and incorporate funny remarks and jokes into your production.

Butterfly land

Topics
Minibeasts.

Starting point
This role-play links up well with a topic on 'Insects' or 'Minibeasts'. The story of *The Very Hungry Caterpillar* by Eric Carle would make a good accompaniment to this role-play and could even be used as the outline for a class production or assembly.

What you need
Gauzy butterfly wings which can be made from painted net curtains attached to wrists and back of neck (see illustration); headbands with springy antennae (available at seaside gift shops, etc.); sleeping bags or other large sacks with elastic around the top, loose enough to go around a waist and decorated along the sides to look like caterpillars (see illustration); plastic eggs from the role-play shop; different shades of sugar paper and tissue-paper to make flowers; scissors, adhesive, sticky tape.

What to do
Create a caterpillar-and-butterfly world by putting large leaves and flowers on the wall of the role-play area. Try to make them in proportion to your child-caterpillars and make some of them protrude from the walls to give a 3-D effect. Children can then pretend to eat the leaves. When they are ready, they can pupate for a while and then emerge as butterflies. This requires some planning as the butterfly wings will have to be put on before climbing into the caterpillar sack. Once the butterfly has laid its eggs on a leaf, the whole cycle can start again.

If a full performance based on *The Very Hungry Caterpillar* is required, you will need pictures of all the different things he ate. It is possible to have children play the parts of, for instance, two plums. They should have a card flap which could be removed when the caterpillar has eaten a hole through the fruit.

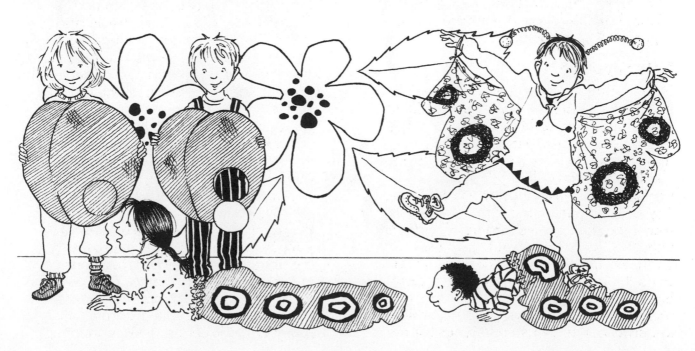

Television land

Topics
The media; Communications.

Starting point
During the topic of 'Ourselves' it became clear that children in our class spent many hours at home watching television and videos rather than playing games. We decided to use their knowledge of TV characters to stimulate some role-play.

What you need
Any available costumes relating to children's TV characters. Green tabards are a must for the Ninja Turtles, as are accompanying headbands. She-ra, Batman and Spiderman outfits are widely available from toy shops. You may find that some of the children have such costumes at home and do not mind bringing them into school for other children to enjoy. If you do not teach in an area where this is likely to happen, black 'Batman' capes are easily made from an old skirt unpicked down one seam and some tape attached to form a tie at what was the waist. The same can be done with a red skirt for a Spiderman cape.

Australian television 'soaps' can be catered for with Bermuda shorts, swimsuits and T-shirts. Characters from *Thunderbirds* need tabards or use sashes.

What to do
Encourage the children to play their favourite characters in the role-play corner. There will probably be bizarre combinations of Batman meets Turtles meets Neighbours, but the children will be able to use their own imagination with these familiar characters, instead of just accepting what the television has to offer.

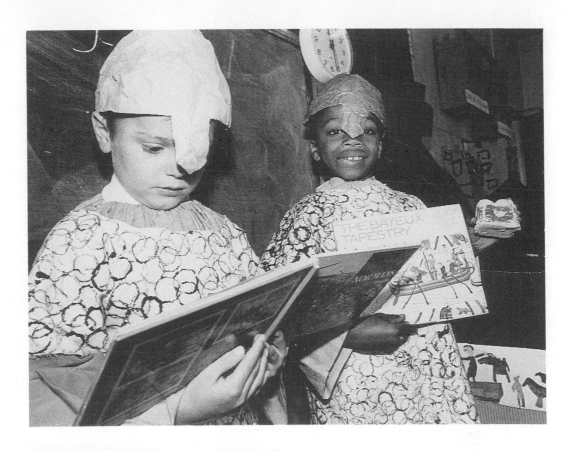

Role-play for history and geography

Chapter nine

History and geography are now compulsory foundation subjects in Years 1 and 2 of Key Stage 1. These subjects should be treated in the same way as any other subject in early-years teaching. Children learn best by being given learning experiences which enable them to develop skills. Role-play is an ideal way of teaching children to empathise with people from the past or from cultures other than their own.

If some of these activities seem over-simplified, it is to enable children to grasp the basic differences between themselves and the characters they are playing, which they need to do if they are to work towards the sort of knowledge expected of them in Key Stage 2.

Life in the Stone Age

Topics
Prehistory.

Starting point
Tell the children some stories based on the lives of the Stone Age people. The Trog stories published by E. J. Arnold are ideal for this. Discuss what it must have been like living in the cave, with no light except for firelight and sunlight, no metals, just stones, wood, animal hides and bones to make everything you need.

What you need
Leather (imitation leather will do) or fur-fabric tabards; strong cardboard 'knives' and 'axes'; stones of various sorts — flints if you have them; sticks and offcuts of wood; 'fire' made of wood, and red and yellow acetate; straw and leaves for bedding; a 'cave' made from a large cardboard box with a hole cut out, painted by the children to look like rock; paint, paintbrushes, scissors; clay or Plasticine (optional).

What to do
Banish all plastic and metal objects from the role-corner. Provide tasks for your Stone Age people: moving a heavy weight, for instance, or making a container to carry water. You should stress that Stone Age people had to make everything they needed as there was no popping down to the shops!

The children usually show a great deal of ingenuity in their play, providing themselves with some of the basic utensils and making furniture from wood, straw and stone.

Pirates

Topics
The sea; Outlaws.

Starting point
Ask the children what they know about pirates. Many will have seen films such as *Hook*, so you could read some extracts from J. M. Barrie's classic or from the Walt Disney book-of-the-film.

What you need
Pirate costumes — cloaks, waistcoats, hats, scarves, eye patches, plastic swords and daggers; a gangplank (on the floor), a big box for a boat, a sail, a pirate flag, a treasure chest (a box with some costume jewellery), paint, paintbrushes, scissors.

What to do
Decorating the box to look like a boat could be a class project and many adventures and sea rescues will take place in the role-corner while the theme is 'Pirates'.

   If a performance is required, you could teach your children any of the following songs (this is aimed at reception-class children.)

1. (To the tune of 'Frère Jaques'):

   We are pirates, we are pirates,
   Yo ho ho, yo ho ho,
   See our skull and cross-bones, see our
      skull and cross-bones,
   yo ho ho, yo ho ho.
   We go sailing, we go sailing,
   On the sea, on the sea,
   Looking out for treasure, looking out
      for treasure,
   For you and me, for you and me.

   This is sung as the pirates come on to the stage area, carrying or dragging the treasure chest.

2. (To the tune of 'The bear went over the mountain')

The pirates went over the mountain,
   the pirates went over the mountain,
The pirates went over the mountain, to
   see what they could see.
But all that they could see, but all that
   they could see
Was the other side of the mountain, the
   other side of the mountain,
The other side of the mountain was all
   that they could see.
So they went back over the mountain,
   etc.

During this song the pirates walk from one side of the stage to the other, shading their eyes and looking into the distance. Then they do the same coming back. This can be repeated as often as your audience can bear it.

3. (To the tune of 'If you're happy and you know it')

Verse 1
If you're a pirate and you know it, clap
   your hands.

Verse 2
If you're going to look for treasure,
   stamp your feet.
   [Repeat]
If you're going to look for treasure,
   even in the stormy weather,
If you're going to look for treasure,
   stamp your feet.

The actions speak for themselves in the above.

4. For the following song, ten pirates should line up.

Ten little pirates standing in a line.
One walked the plank and then there
   were nine.
Nine little pirates got up very late.
A cannon ball hit one and then there
   were eight.
Eight little pirates sailing down to
   Devon,
One drank too much rum and then
   there were seven.
Seven little pirates playing silly tricks,
One tied himself in knots and then
   there were six.
Six little pirates going for a dive,
A big fish swallowed one and then
   there were five.
Five littles pirates landing on the shore,

A coconut hit one and then there were
   four.
Four little pirates sailing out to sea,
One fell overboard and then there
   were three.
Three little pirates cooking up a stew,
One fell in and then there were two.
Two little pirates sitting in the sun,
One got frizzled up and then there
   was one.
One little pirate feeling all alone,
He found treasure (Hurray!) and then
   there were none.

   As each pirate is eliminated, he or she should collapse on the floor. You could also get your pirates to groan or gurgle loudly when it is their turn. They can all jump up and cheer when the last pirate finds the treasure.

A castle

Topics
Medieval life; Houses and homes.

Starting point
Most children have some idea of royalty. There are lots of stories such as 'The Sleeping Beauty' and 'Robin Hood' which are based on life as it was lived in a medieval castle. Other stories of knights in armour are also good starting points. There are also modern stories, for example, *I Want My Potty* by Tony Ross, set in the environment of a castle.

What you need
Photographs of different sorts of castles; large sheets of thick paper, card and foil; a large supply of sticky tape; black felt-tipped pens; costumes to suit your type of castle — we concentrated on a fairy-tale castle, so we needed lots of lacy dresses (old nighties were excellent) and head-dresses made from a cone of gold card with a gauzy scarf at the end (see illustration).

You will also need crowns made of gold card, and lots of tabards and tights for the servants, kings and princes.

What to do
Talk about what a castle looks like and show a few pictures. Let the children discuss and decide which sort of castle they want to make — a 'real' or a fairy-tale one. Once this decision has been taken, encourage the children to design their own castle. Let them draw plans of how they want it to look, which can then be amalgamated into a master plan. A fairy-tale castle can easily be made using gold foil, whereas a more realistic one would require large sheets of grey paper and black paint for masonry joints.

The children should try to build their castle in their own way. This will enable them to discover that turrets are difficult to fix on to the castle walls and they will go through lots of sticky tape trying to fit conical roofs on to towers. But it will be their own castle, which they have made to play in, and whatever it looks like to an adult, they will think it is wonderful.

A Victorian music hall

Topics
Sound; Theatre; The Victorians.

Starting point
Talk about a music hall with your class. Some of the children may have seen scenes from a music hall in a film or on TV, which may help them to understand that before there was TV or cinema, people used to be entertained by live performers singing and telling jokes on stage. There may even be an old variety theatre in your town which has probably seen several transformations into a cinema, a bowling alley or a bingo hall.

What you need
Costumes are essential for that 'Old Time' look: waistcoats, bow ties, braces, top hats, black jackets; flat caps, trousers cut short and gathered into breeches; a large mallet for the Master of Ceremonies; striped blazers, boaters (see illustration) and a cloak; borrowed bridesmaids' dresses with frilly underskirts; muffs, big floppy hats, bonnets, feather boas; a bearskin (for strongman) and papier-mâché weights for him to lift; foam balls for jugglers; large plastic noses for clowns; face paints; a cassette player with tapes of music-hall songs, for example, 'Any old iron', 'My old man said "follow the van"', 'If you were the only girl in the world', 'The Lambeth Walk'; paper, coloured paper, card, paint, glue, scissors.

What to do
Create a stage area (preferably slightly raised), with some chairs for the audience. Encourage the children to do 'turns' on stage for their friends. Ask them to decorate the wall to look like a real theatre arch and to make posters informing the audience of the treats in store.

1 Cut strip of card adjusted to circumference of child's head. glue

2 Draw round inside of strip onto oval of card.

3 Cut out, leaving tabs for gluing on inside.

4 Glue together and put paper band on.

The jungle

Topics

Animals; Plants; Life in other lands.

Starting point

There is a very good song called 'Walking through the jungle' in the book *Game-songs with Professor Dogg's Troupe* published by A. & C. Black. This would make a good starting point for this role-play.

What you need

A Tarzan costume and sarongs; a swinging rope and PE mats; lots of fabric, paper and/or card in varying shades of green; large artificial or real potted plants; old tights dyed green and stuffed with newspaper to look like vines; brightly coloured paper and tissue-paper for making flowers and butterflies; Cromar paint, ordinary paint and paintbrushes; a stapler, scissors, a staple gun, sticky tape, string, adhesive.

What to do

Ask each child to cut a large green leaf out of green card or paper. Those who need lots of practice with cutting could try to cut some long creepers and it really does not matter if they cut lumps off by accident as these can all be stapled on to the display.

The class should also design and make some exotic flowers. Butterflies can be made by folding paper, squirting Cromar paint on one side and smoothing it into a butterfly shape. If two or more colours are used, you will have a most attractive shiny butterfly.

Drape the green fabric on paper over the display area. Any shade will do and different shades can overlap. Folds and tucks in the fabric will give more of a 3-D effect. Attach creepers, leaves and vines.

Old tights dyed green give a really good effect when they are stretched or stuffed to make lumpy vines. Put the flowers and butterflies over the greenery and there you have a jungle. You could now ask the children to paint some jungle animals which could then seem to be peeping out from behind the foliage.

Once the role-play area has been decorated, it needs to be played in. Encourage the children to imagine surviving in the jungle and making friends with the animals. If you attach a rope to the ceiling so that Tarzan can swing, that will be very popular. The children will need close supervision and some PE mats underneath to avoid accidents caused by over-enthusiasm.

Who shall we be today?

Chapter ten

Young children are constantly being told that they are 'too little' to do a great many things they perceive as interesting and exciting. In order to do many of these things in real life, they would need special talents and skills, as well as the time to develop them, and a lot of luck.

Fortunately, imagination can supply anything a child needs. In the role-play area everyone is a star.

Pop stars and disco dancers

Topics
Sound; The media.

Starting point
A discussion of favourite songs and favourite dances will obviously lead to performances. Talk about how we could create a role-play area for singing and dancing. What could it be called?

What you need
A cassette recorder, preferably portable rather than a plug-in one; recordings of the children's favourite songs mentioned in the discussion — include favourite hymns and nursery rhymes, as well as popular tunes. Dances such as the 'Hokey Cokey' and 'The birdie dance' could be interspersed with ballet music, a brass band and pop tunes; a hand-held microphone (an old real one or made from a cardboard tube); a small raised stage would be nice but is not essential; an area for dancing, decorated with aluminium foil; suitable costumes for a pop star or a dancer (lots of glitter and costume jewellery); Flashing lights would be wonderful if they were child-proof like real disco lights. See if you can borrow them from a disco, if only for a short time.

What to do
Prepare a background for the stage area. Strips of aluminium foil dangling down the wall are appropriate for both stage and dancing area. Then let the children perform to their hearts' content, either miming to records or singing on their own. Provide a blank tape so that children who want to record their own singing can do so.

Teachers and pupils

Topics
Ourselves; People who help us.

Starting point
Read *Mr Tick the Teacher* by Allan Ahlberg (Young Puffin Books). Talk about what it is like to be a teacher. Ask the children what they think you do as a teacher.

What you need
An easel, chalkboard and chalk; tables, desks and chairs; blank exercise books or sheets of paper; red felt-tipped pens or Biros; pencils, pencil sharpeners, erasers, paper-clips; several spectacle frames (without lenses) for the 'teachers'; a notice-board; briefcases or large bags for the 'teachers'; stars, merit badges or stickers (rationed).

What to do
Encourage the 'teachers' to help the 'class' to do some work in the exercise books and/or on sheets of paper. The 'teachers' can then mark the work with a red Biro and choose especially good work to be displayed on the notice-board, decorated with a sticker or a star. It is fascinating to listen to this role-play, as children's perceptions of teachers as adults with the power to bestow rewards and punishments is sometimes a shock. Are we *really* that bossy?

Animals galore

Topics
Pets; At the zoo.

Starting point
Ask your class to tell you what they know about one particular animal, for instance, a cat. Read *Today I Am a Cat* by Jane Bottomley (Belitha Press). Talk about what it would be like to be an animal. What animal would the children want to be?

What you need
A cassette recorder and recordings of animal stories; masks or hats with ears (see page 15); costumes — these could be leotards in any suitable colour with a tail attached to the seat or tabards with animal markings painted on; boxes big enough for at least one child to curl up inside, to make a den; paint and paintbrushes.

What to do
Encourage the children to pretend that they are animals of their choice. Provide paint, brushes and blank masks so that they can design their own animal faces. They can then paint their dens to suit the chosen animals. Children encounter many talking animals in their storybooks, so perhaps they would like to act out some of the stories they know. Record a cassette for them of some of these stories, such as 'The lion and the mouse', but do not forget modern stories, for example, *Baby Goz* by Stephen Weatherill (F. Lincoln Ltd), which children will love to listen to while they act out the parts.

As a development of this activity, you could read *I Wish That I Had Duck Feet* by Theo Sieg (HarperCollins) to the children. Could they design their own creature that resembles the mixed-up animal like the 'Which-what-who'?

What to do

Let the children create their own hospital environment in the role-play area. Encourage the use of clipboards for writing down patients' names and temperature.

Make sure that doctors and nurses are of both sexes. To make this point, you could sing a version of 'Miss Polly had a dolly' where the doctor comes with *her* bag and *her* hat. It is amazing how indignant some of the boys get, pointing out to you that you've 'got it wrong'.

Doctors and nurses

Topics

People who help us; Look after yourself.

Starting point

Ask if anyone has been to hospital lately. Read *Miss Dose the Doctor's Daughter* by Allan Ahlberg (Young Puffin Books). Discuss what happens when we go to hospital. Who looks after us most of the time? Who is going to be a doctor when they grow up? Who is going to be a nurse?

What you need

White coats and caps (white shirts and white card headbands will do); stethoscopes, syringes, bandages, etc. (Fisher Price doctor's set is good); a bed and some chairs; empty clean plastic bottles of disinfectant; clipboards with paper and pens attached; a trolley.

The conjuror

Topics

Magic and mystery; Clever people.

Starting point

Talk about magicians and conjurors. The children may have seen conjuring acts on the television. Read *Mr Cosmo the Conjuror* by Allan Ahlberg (Young Puffin Books). A visit from a real conjuror would, of course be the perfect starting point.

What you need

A top hat, a black cape and a false moustache; soft toys to produce from the hat — rabbit, parrot, chicken, etc.; a 'Magic Tricks' set — a disappearing egg, a magic wand, playing cards, a ring, fine silk scarves, coins; activity paper, paper, paint, paintbrushes, felt-tipped pens, scissors.

What to do

Demonstrate some easy tricks to the children, for example, pulling previously hidden scarves or toys out of the hat. Show them the 'Magic Tricks' set — pretend to find a coin or a card behind a

child's ear, etc. Then let the children themselves take over the role-play area, designing a suitable backdrop for their performance. Obviously, there will need to be large notices announcing the Great Cosmo or Marvo and their wonderful tricks. Hand-written leaflets could also be distributed throughout the school.

In the television studio

Topics
The media; Communications.

Starting point
Ask the children if they have seen the evening news or a chat show recently. How many people do they think are in the studio? A visit to a real studio, though obviously difficult to arrange, would be an excellent experience for the children.

What you need
A table and some chairs, as on a chat-show set — one chair should have a replaceable label which can be changed each time a different child takes up the role; a 'camera' made from a cardboard box set on cardboard-tube legs and painted black; similarly made 'spotlights'; a clapper-board made from stiff card, with a paper fastener for a hinge (see illustration); paper and pencils.

What to do
Encourage the children to script their favourite television and video scenes, as well as writing their own original efforts. Scripts should, of course, be legible, otherwise the actors will be unable to speak the correct words. Children can take turns to be their favourite character or a chat-show host(ess). They can then sit on the other side of the camera as the director or a camera operator.

Appendix 1

The Chapatti Man

Once there was a woman who had seven hungry little children. To feed them, she made a huge bowl of chapatti dough and rolled it into one enormous chapatti. Then she put it into the pan to cook. When the chapatti was cooked on one side, the mother flipped it over to cook on the other side. But the chapatti jumped out of the pan on his little legs and said:

'Run, run as fast as you can, you can't catch me, I'm the Chapatti Man!'

The Chapatti Man ran out of the house and after him ran the mother and the seven hungry little children.

Along the road, the Chapatti Man met an elephant.

'Stop, little Chapatti Man,' trumpeted the elephant, 'I want to eat you!' 'Oh, no', said the Chapatti Man, 'I have run away from a mother and seven hungry little children, and I can run away from YOU!' Run, run as fast as you can, you can't catch me, I'm the Chapatti Man.'

So he ran on and along the road he met a cow.

'Stop, little Chapatti Man, I want to eat you, mooed the cow.

'Oh, no,' said the Chapatti Man, 'I have run away from a mother and seven hungry little children, I have run away from an elephant and I can run away from YOU! Run, run as fast as you can, you can't catch me, I'm the Chapatti Man!'

So he ran on and along the road he met a horse.

'Stop, little Chapatti Man,' neighed the horse, 'I want to eat you.'

'Oh, no,' said the Chapatti Man, 'I have run away from a mother and seven hungry little children, I have run away from an elephant, I have run away from a cow and I can run away from YOU! Run, run as fast as you can, you can't catch me, I'm the Chapatti Man!'

So he ran on and along the road he met a tiger.

'Stop, little Chapatti Man,' growled the tiger, 'I want to eat you.'

'Oh, no,' said the Chapatti Man, 'I have run away from a mother and seven hungry little children, I have run away from an elephant, I have run away from a cow, I have run away from a horse and I can run away from YOU! Run, run as fast as you can, you can't catch me, I'm the Chapatti Man!'

The Chapatti Man ran on and soon he came to a river. Sitting by the river bank was a wise old monkey. He saw the Chapatti Man and knew he could not cross the river by himself.

'Hello, little Chapatti Man,' he said, 'Can I help you to cross the river?'

'Yes please,' said the Chapatti Man.

'Why don't you sit on my head, little Chapatti Man,' said the monkey, 'and I will swim across the river.'

So the Chapatti Man climbed on to the monkey's head and the monkey began to swim across the river. Halfway across, the monkey said, 'This river is very deep. I am worried about you getting wet, little Chapatti Man. Jump down on to my nose to keep dry.'

The Chapatti Man climbed on to the monkey's nose and then, with a great big gulp, the wise monkey swallowed the Chapatti Man before they reached the other side of the river.

That was the end of the Chapatti Man. The mother and the seven hungry little children, and the elephant, and the cow, and the horse, and the tiger, all went hungry to bed. But the wise monkey had eaten all of the Chapatti Man and he wasn't hungry at all.

Appendix 2

The golden goose (The princess who could not smile)

Once upon a time there was a king who was very worried about his daughter. The princess could not smile and had never laughed like an ordinary girl. The king was very worried about her, so he proclaimed throughout the land that the first man to make his daughter smile should marry her and inherit half his kingdom.

On the other side of the kingdom lived a boy called Jack. He was a very kind boy and always tried to help people in need. One day Jack was chopping wood when an old woman came along. She was crying and seemed very upset.

'Whatever is the matter?' asked Jack. 'Can I do anything to help?'

'I'm so hungry,' said the old woman, 'I haven't eaten for three days.'

Now Jack had some food with him. It was not much and it was all he had to eat for that day. But he was such a kind boy that he gave all his food to the old woman.

When she had eaten, the old woman thanked Jack and told him to look for his reward in the hollow of a nearby tree.

Jack looked in the hollow tree and there was the most wonderful goose with golden feathers. 'I must take this to show the king,' thought Jack. But the minute he took hold of the goose, his hands stuck fast to it and he could not let go.

'Oh, well,' thought Jack, 'I'll go and see the king anyway.' And off he went.

The first place Jack came to was a farm.

'What a beautiful goose,' said the farmer's daughter. 'Can I have just one feather?'

Jack, who was a kind boy, said she could have a feather from the golden goose. But as soon as the farmer's daughter touched the feather, her hand stuck fast to the goose and she could not let go. She called to her mother for help, but when her mother touched her, she, too, stuck fast and could not let go. So the mother called for her husband to help her. When the farmer came, he got hold of his wife to pull her away, but he, too, stuck fast and could not let go.

So there they were: Jack, the farmer's daughter, the farmer's wife and the farmer, all stuck fast to the golden goose.

'Well, I'm still going to see the king,' said Jack, 'And it looks like you are all coming with me!'

The next place they came to was a mill.

'What a beautiful goose,' said the miller's daughter, 'Can I have just one feather?'

'I wouldn't touch it if I were you,' said Jack, but it was too late. The miller's daughter had already touched the farmer. Her hand stuck fast and she could not let go. She called to her friend to help her, but when the friend touched her, she could not let go, either.

Soon they were entering the capital city where the royal palace was and all along the way people were reaching out to touch the golden goose. Now Jack had twenty people stuck in a long line behind his goose.

The king was still worried and the princess had still not smiled when Jack and his golden goose went past the palace windows one morning. When the princess saw all these people stuck together in a long line, tripping over each other and grumbling, a strange thing happened. Her mouth began to curl upwards at the ends. She started to make strange noises in her throat. The king rushed to her, thinking she was ill. Suddenly the princess opened up her mouth and . . . she LAUGHED! She didn't grin, she didn't smile, she laughed until tears ran down her face. Her laughter broke the spell which had held everyone to the golden goose and they were all set free.

The king was very pleased with Jack and, since he had made the princess not just smile, but laugh, he gave him half his kingdom straight away. Jack married the princess and they all lived happily ever after.